Not to be taken into Front Line Trenches.

Issued to include Regimental Commanders.

INSTRUCTION

ON

THE OFFENSIVE ACTION OF LARGE UNITS

IN BATTLE

TRANSLATED FROM THE FRENCH EDITION

OF OCTOBER 31, 1917

AT

HEADQUARTERS AMERICAN EXPEDITIONARY FORCES

FRANCE

—

January, 1918

Published by Books Express Publishing
Copyright © Books Express, 2011
ISBN 978-1-780392-08-0

Books Express publications are available from all good retail and online booksellers. For
publishing proposals and direct ordering please contact us at: info@books-express.com

Not to be taken into Front Line Trenches.
Issued to include Regimental Commanders.

INSTRUCTION

ON

THE OFFENSIVE ACTION OF LARGE UNITS

IN BATTLE

TRANSLATED FROM THE FRENCH EDITION

OF OCTOBER 31, 1917

AT

HEADQUARTERS AMERICAN EXPEDITIONARY FORCES

FRANCE

—

January, 1918

TABLE OF CONTENTS.

PART III.

EXECUTION.

INTRODUCTION.

The battle comprises defensive actions and offensive actions, closely connected with each other.

In the first the Command, while working constantly on the enemy, groups and reorganizes his forces and resources of every kind, in view of the later great attacks.

In the second, he develops the attacks by employing to the full the means that he has collected.

The mission of the Armies in these different periods is fixed by the *secret orders* of the General Commander-in-Chief.

Defensives actions concern themselves with :

Exercising over the enemy a continual action or wearing down and with controlling its results : a *material wearing down,* by the losses that we try to inflict on him, while economizing our own resources to the maximum; and a *moral wearing down,* resulting from these very losses and from the threat of attack under which we must constantly hold the enemy.

Studying and effectively preparing along the entire front offensive actions which will have for their object either making a breach in the hostile front by force or advancing in contact with the enemy if the latter falls back.

Thus *offensive actions* must, at the time and in the zones chosen by the command, be launched with a suddenness and a variety which will make it possible to take the enemy by surprise.

All the Armies must be ready to profit by the confusion produced by these actions in the enemy's general formation.

Offensive actions will first take the form of attacks on definite and limited objectives. These attacks will be renewed and varied, in the minimum of time and maximum of space, until they have produced a breach in the enemy's fortifications. They will lead to operations with more and more distant aims, in which the decision of the battle and the pursuit of the hostile army will be successively considered.

Consequently, the Armies must :

Organize themselves defensively, in order to economize their own forces constantly and to guarantee the inviolability of the front by the full use of firing power and the resources of fortification.

Echelon themselves in depth, in order to remain constantly ready to maneuver : parade maneuver to deceive the enemy's attacks; maneuver of attack to strike the enemy and to pursue him if he tries to retreat.

Watch and reconnoiter the enemy, on the one hand, to know beforehand his preparations for an offensive, and on the other to find his weak spots and to prepare for ulterior maneuvers.

Execute on well chosen points attacks intended to increase the wearing down of the enemy and to weaken his field works.

Renew and vary these attacks unceasingly, by combining the effects of surprise and powerful offensive means, so as to bring about the disorganization of the enemy and to overcome his resistance.

Prepare, at each phase of every offensive action, the development of the success sought for.

PART I.

PURPOSE AND CONDITIONS OF AN OFFENSIVE ACTION.

———

PART I.

PURPOSE AND CONDITIONS OF AN OFFENSIVE ACTION.

CHAPTER I.

PURPOSE. — GENERAL CONDITIONS.

1. The *aim* of an offensive action is the achievement of moral and material successes, first localized in time, and space, then successively increased and constantly directed toward the accomplishment of a decisive victory.

An offensive action may include several attacks, successive or simultaneous. Each attack may itself last several days and be divided into several phases.

Every attack should insure :

1) The carrying of a part of the terrain occupied by the enemy, with the capture or destruction of the troops and materiel found there.

2) The holding of the ground gained and, if necessary, its methodical development.

2. The High Command defines and specifies the purposes of the offensive action.

The command, in all the echelons concerned in its execution, determines the form of the attacks and regulates the action of the large units in relation to each other.

To this end he takes into account the relative strength of the different objectives and the influence which the maneuvers or advances of one unit may exercise over the maneuvers or advances of a neighboring unit.

The *conditions* essential to the success of an attack are :
Superiority of means.
Surprise.
A complete preparation.

I. — SUPERIORITY OF MEANS.

3. Superiority of means results :

From superiority in troops and materiel, from which is derived superiority of fire.
From the circumstances of the terrain.
From atmospheric conditions.

4. A) Numerical superiority.

This makes it possible to extend the fronts of attacks, to persevere longer in the offensive and to present fresh reserves before a depleted enemy.

5. B) Circumstances of the terrain.

a) **In the rear.** — The command chooses and limits the zones of attack so that the development of communications and installations of the rear may be to his advantage.

b) **On the front of attack.** — In each zone of attack thus determined, the commands of large units charged with carrying them out choose points of attack :
In which the artillery may develop the entire power of its fire.
In which the infantry may profit by all its weapons and may be protected against surprises.
In which terrestrial and aerial observation may be insured and make it possible to obtain concentration of views and of fire.
In which the batteries and tanks may move.

c) **In the zone of the objectives.** — As far as possible, every attack should improve the situation of the assailant and procure for him : good observation posts, emplacements suitable for the installation and operation of the artillery and favorable to infantry fire, defiladed roads and easy communications. These conditions are indispensable for holding the ground gained and for developing later operations. The opposite conditions will be imposed on the enemy so that he may neither counter-attack with any chance of success, nor re-establish himself, nor resist new attacks.

6. C) ATMOSPHERIC CONDITIONS.

The season and the atmospheric conditions exercise a considerable influence over the preparation of the operations as well as over their execution.

Favorable winds make it possible to use gas.

7. It will not always be possible to realize these conditions entirely, especially as far as choice of terrain and atmospheric conditions are concerned. But the command will try to come as near it as possible.

II. — SURPRISE.

8. Surprise may be either strategic or tactical.

a) **Strategic surprise** may be achieved when an attack is launched, after a rapid and secret preparation, on a terrain on which the enemy can not, in the necessary time :

Either bring up his general reserves (artillery, aviation, infantry).

Or execute preventive maneuvers (advance or retreat of forces).

To obtain it at a given place and time, the High Command will usually multiply and vary offensive actions in space as well as in time (*).

b) **Tactical surprise** consists in surprising the enemy

(*) In certain cases, the endeavor to accomplish strategic surprise will be the prime factor in the preparation of an offensive action.

by the choice of the precise moment and front of attack
and in submerging him by the rapidity of the execution,
so that he may employ neither his fire nor his local reserves
in the proper conditions.

It is an essential factor of success in any attack.

The commanders in all echelons must respect and impose
secrecy.

Distribution of written orders must be strictly limited
to the units or services concerned : the most severe penalties
are imposed for any negligence in this matter.

The Staffs must not furnish to the services a complete
order, but an *extract* containing only what it is indispensable
for them to know.

III — THE PREPARATION.

9. *The preparation is the sum of the measures having for
their object the bringing into action of the means of attack
and the destruction or neutralization of the means of defense.* It includes :

A) The preparation of the command and the troops.

B) The establishment of plans and offensive works.

C) The collection of means and destructions.

10. A) THE PREPARATION OF THE COMMAND AND THE
TROOPS.

The command and the staffs of all the large units on the
front must always hold themselves *ready*, must consider
and study all the hypotheses of attack in their sector,
must make a detailed study of the enemy's formation, of
his defensive organizations and his artillery system. Thus
the delays in the preparatory works will be reduced to a
minimum for the command and the staffs of the units
assigned to an offensive action on any zone whatever of
the front.

The officers apply themselves unceasingly to *raising the
morale* of their troops and to improving the discipline,
training and instruction. They see to the material installation, the hygiene, rest and food of their men.

The infantry, while it is kept in the rear, prepares itself for the role which will fall to it. It reconnoiters the terrain on which it will be called to act; it studies relief maps, photographs, panoramic sketches and maps of all sorts. It rehearses the attack on specially prepared grounds.

In all arms and in all echelons, the officers and the troops will increase their confidence in success by ascertaining the importance of the means brought into action, and by observing the intensity of the bombardment and the efficacy of the artillery preparation.

They must be brought to the point of *desiring the attack.*

11. B) Drawing up of plans. — Offensive works.

The first part of the preparation of an offensive action comprises the drawing up of plans and the execution of offensive works.

The *plans* are first drawn up in outline by the local command (group of armies, army) for the large units destined to carry out the operation. They are then filled out in detail by these large units themselves when they have carried out their reconnoitering and are ready to set to work.

The *offensive works* are commenced as soon as the plans are drawn up in outline.

As soon as possible the command insures the bringing up of all the means that circumstances make it possible to collect in advance (artillery, aeronautics, materiel, etc...).

The more this early preparation has been carried out, the more possible it will be to surprise the enemy, especially if the sectors of attack preserve their usual appearance during the last weeks before the attack.

12. C) Collection of means. — Destructions.

The second part of the preparation must be as brief as possible, in order to surprise the enemy.

It includes :

The installation and, if necessary, the trial fire of all the artillery units which it has been impossible to bring up during the first part of the preparation.

The installation and the reconnaissance or combats of the aeronautic units in the same case.

The transport of large units, tanks, or various troops destined for the offensive action, their assembling in the rear of the sectors of attack, their reconnaissances, their special training in the plan of engagement and, according to these reconnaissances, the finishing of the works.

The methodical destruction of the enemy's means by artillery and aircraft, in case the effort to secure surprise is not the main element of the preparation.

The bringing up of the infantry.

At the beginning of the second part, it will still be possible to conceal a part of the preparations from the enemy, if all precautions are taken to regulate the circulation, if the movements are carried out almost exclusively at night, if the command insists on a judicious use of camouflage, and if the trial fire of the artillery and the aerial reconnaissance or combats are very methodically regulated.

From the moment that the aviation develops its air battles and the artillery begins its destruction fires, the enemy knows that the attack is about to be launched.

It will then be the duty of the command (group of armies or army) to reduce to the minimum the delays in preparation by taking account of the following fact :

The chances for success lie as much in surprise and in neutralization at the moment of attack as in the complete destruction of the enemy's batteries, organizations and observation posts.

CHAPTER II.

CONDITIONS FOR THE USE AND DISTRIBUTION OF FORCES AND MEANS.

(LARGE UNITS. — INFANTRY.)

13. The general principles which form the subject of Chapter II must not be considered as rigid formulae : there is no formula which will relieve the commanders from planning and directing the battle.

I. — CHOICE OF OBJECTIVES AND CALCULATION OF THE NECESSARY FORCES AND MEANS.

14. The enemy's defensive system consists in a series of positions echelonned in depth, either completely organized or simply prepared.

It is idle to think of making in this system, at a single effort, a breach wide enough to bring about the disorganization of the whole.

Hence the offensive action will be characterized by successive attacks.

15. Each one of the enemy's positions, with the batteries situated near it, constitutes the natural objective of a determined attack. In fact, it is possible :

To prepare the attack of the position completely by the artillery or to open up ways for the infantry by the crushing action of the tanks.

To make sure that the infantry is closely accompanied by the artillery in the course of its advance to attack.

To consider the possibility of advancing beyond the position carried : an advance which will bring the infantry close enough to attack the following position; which will allow the infantry to capture or destroy important hostile materiel, to increase the number of prisoners and thus to disorganize the enemy's defensive system; which finally may be effectively covered by the artillery without its being necessary to execute at the beginning of the attack important displacements of the batteries.

16. Each of these attacks must be intrusted to large units having a sufficient offensive capacity in depth (2000 to 3500 meters) to carry it through from beginning to end.

After this effort it will generally be necessary to :

Pass or *relieve* the large units that have attacked in the first line.

To execute displacements of artillery.

17. Finally, as a general rule and especially at the beginning of an offensive action, each attack will aim, as far as depth is concerned :

a) To carry a hostile position.

b) To advance beyond that, within attacking distance of the following position.

c) To capture or destroy the enemy's batteries situated on the terrain of the advance thus accomplished, either by the main body of the attack, or by reconnaissance or advanced detachments.

Nevertheless, the command must consider the possibility of a success beyond the limit of the attack planned, in case the enemy, surprised, yields ground rapidly and an immediate advance would allow us to occupy important points abandonned by him, before he could recover.

The conditions of such an advance are indicated below, in the definition of objectives. Its mechanism will be studied in the third part.

Definition of objectives.

18. *a*) The **normal objective** of every attack is the line which the attacking troops must reach at the limits of the terrain that the command wishes to take from the enemy and for the conquest of which he brings into action the entire resources of his artillery. This normal objective is therefore determined by the artillery possibilities and, in certain cases, by the possibility of the action of the tanks.

b) An **intermediate objective** is a temporary halt provided for a given moment in the advance with a view to facilitating the re-formation of the infantry and the adjusting of the artillery barrage. In the choice of intermediate objectives one must take into account the prime necessity of insuring to the command and to the artillery observation posts giving extensive views over the zone of further advance, and to procure for the reserve troops (and in case of necessity for the batteries) the zone of maneuver which is indispensable to them in order to effect their displacements out of sight of the enemy.

c) The **possible objective** is a line which the troops may reach beyond the normal objective if the combat develops favorably, within the limits provided by the command, which must always remain master of the depth of the advance of the attack.

No special artillery preparation must be executed with a view to the conquest of such an objective.

But destructions or neutralizations will often have been executed on observation posts, flanking positions or distant works; and, by that very fact, they may contribute to annihilating the enemy's force of resistance beyond the normal objective.

The notion of an advance toward an objective called possible corresponds to a possibility frequently met with on battle fields.

Therefore the command must provide for and regulate this possible advance, especially as far as concerns :

The march of the infantry.

The support of the infantry by accompanying artillery fire.

The throwing forward of communications and liaisons, of batteries, of materiel and of provisions.

d) The **advance beyond the possible objective** is defined by the designation of distant *points of direction*, to insure the proper orientation of efforts and axes of liaison along which will be established *centers of information* for the transmission of information and orders.

This advance beyond the possible objective is also provided for in the plans, *but it must be entered on only by the authorization of the command, who alone seeing the entire situation, is alone capable of judging of the chances of success* (see Chapter IX).

Simultaneousness of attacks.

19. Along the entire front of an offensive action a simultaneousness in the launching of the first attacks will facilitate the achievement of tactical surprise and the carrying of the first objectives.

For the later attacks it will usually be well to divide the front into broad sections, each including the operation of several large units, so that each section may lend itself to the execution of an attack while the others are bringing up their means. On the other hand, as the permanence of artillery action will be assured in all these sections, the enemy will be constantly attacked and threatened everywhere without his having the leisure to launch counter-attacks or concentrations of fire with any knowledge of the situation.

Thus the necessity of limiting the attacks in space and echellonning them in time in no wise excludes the possibility of continuity, which it is always profitable to insure to them.

Succession of attacks.

20. When the offensive action includes the development of several attacks, the intervals of time separating two attacks in each section of the offensive front should be reduced to the minimum.

These intervals are a function of :

The development of communications (trails, roads, narrow gauge railways, etc...) and liaison.

The displacement of the artillery.

The bringing up of materiel and provisions of all sorts.

The modifications to be made in the infantry formation (advance of the infantry division, transfer of the command posts and observation posts).

Artillery preparation and the bringing up of the tanks for the later assault.

It takes a long time to carry out these various operations after a considerable advance, and in this case it may happen that the later attack will be launched several weeks after the preceding one.

The enemy then has time to reorganize and reëstablish himself.

So long a delay is absolutely inadmissible.

No more than a few days must be allowed to elapse between successive attacks.

To this end each attack must ordinarily aim at carrying one hostile position only.

Calculation of the necessary forces and means.

21. The calculation of forces and means to be brought into action and the choice of objectives are intimately connected and constantly react on each other.

In the beginning, the plan of operations leads to the choice of objectives that it is desirable to attain.

Sometimes the successive calculation of available forces and means necessitates a restriction of these objectives and sometimes it authorizes their extension.

If unforeseen incidents arise, *the commander uses every means to keep his freedom of action* and to preserve his available troops. He should not fear *to push to the point of risk the economy of forces and means on all points that are of secondary interest for him,* in order to preserve his own plan intact.

II. — LARGE UNITS.

22. The forces and means devoted to an offensive action constitute temporary groups.

These groups are *organized* so that the action may be

carried out with method, order, rapidity and continuity, conditions necessary to all success : they form the *Large Units*, including a command and a variable proportion of the different arms.

The Command.

23. The **command** organizes and directs the attacks.

a) As to organization, he pays the greatest attention to the drawing up of the *plans*, which must be essentially practical, precise and adapted to the needs and possibilities of maneuver of the organs of execution.

These plans are studied in the different hierarchic echelons of each large unit and brought into accord with those of the neighboring units.

They are afterward put into working condition by orders that confirm or complete them.

b) As to the direction of the attacks, the command endeavors to carry out his general plans, while taking into account the incidents of battle and all the new circumstances which may necessitate instantaneous decisions.

A commander must never hesitate to assume responsability and to act on his own initiative, to insure the success of his own operations as well as to come to the aid of the neighboring units.

During the battle he stays in a place where he can exercise all his functions.

The command is seconded by *staff officers* who work in the name of their commander and seek to furnish him the elements of his decisions, in the course of their functions with the troops as well as by the studies confided to them. These officers anticipate the requests of the troops and see that they are granted.

The different arms.

24. All arms, whatever their manner of grouping, concur in the development of the battle.

The command insures their material and moral *liaison :* this is his most important function.

25. A) The INFANTRY, after the artillery or the tanks have opened the way, and under the cover of artillery and machine gun fire, conquer the terrain, occupy it, clean it up, organize it and preserve it.

The infantry must aid the arms working for its benefit, must facilitate their installation, insure their provisioning and help in their displacements.

It is powerfully armed to destroy by its own tools the obstacles which may have escaped the artillery action of destruction and neutralization, and to insure the preservation of the conquered terrain.

26. The machine guns are capable of bringing the most valuable aid to the infantry.

In the development of an attack, their role is double :

a) Immediate accompanying of the infantry units of which they form a part, to support them in their advance and to insure their resistance in the positions attained.

b) Distant action by direct or indirect fire under the form of wearing down fire, fixed barrages or concentrations.

Indirect fire produces appreciable effects only in massed action ; it is confided to groups of *machine guns* whose organization is the object of special provision by the command.

27. B) The ARTILLERY opens the way to the infantry by breaking down the obstacles which oppose its march, that is the enemy's artillery and organizations.

It is always ready to precede and to cover the infantry by its fires, to protect its advance as well as to guard it against attacks and counter-attacks during its halts.

It neutralizes by fire and gas all of the enemy's means that may have escaped its destructive fire.

It prevents the enemy from bringing up supplies and establishing himself during a halt by fire on his trenches, communications and his rear, on his reinforcements, reliefs, extra materiel and ammunitions, and by executing frequent fires with gas shells during the preparation as well as during the execution of the attacks.

It organizes its displacements so as to be always ready to fulfil these various missions whatever be the advance of the infantry.

28. C) The AERONAUTIC SERVICE fights to bring about the destruction of the enemy's air service, to insure the free exercise of aerial observation and to prevent it on the part of the enemy. To this end it attacks the enemy's avions, aviation centers and balloons.

By the ubiquity, the continuity and the vigor of its attacks, it creates in front of our lines a permanence of danger for the hostile aviation and a zone of relative security for our observation planes.

It keeps the command informed of the enemy's movements, defensive organizations and installations of all sorts, on the situation of friendly troops, on the degree of completion of the works and their visibility; to this end it makes great and rapid use of photography.

It intervenes in the terrestrial combat by systematically bombarding the enemy's weak points situated out of range of the heavy artillery and by catching under its fires the enemy's infantry and artillery.

It participates in the ranging of artillery of all calibres.

During the battle it insures liaison between the large units and between the different arms, in particular between the infantry and artillery, between the command and the troops.

For these different functions it has at its disposal :

Combat groups and bombardment groups.

Squadrons and balloons for observation, liaison and ranging.

29. D) The ENGINEERS fight and insure the execution of works assigned to them.

Their role in the combat consists of :

The accompanying of the assaulting troops to carry out the destructions which require a technical instruction superior to that of the infantry pioneers.

And, in case of necessity, mine attacks.

But the greater part of the engineer units will always be employed to establish communications and to prolong them over the conquered terrain.

Ordinarily the engineers will not suffice for this task. In that case they will be reinforced by units of other arms, which will be employed under the direction of the engineer commanders of the large units. The engineer companies will be assigned to the works which present especial technical difficulties.

Engineer units must not be broken up : the principle of tactical units applies to the engineers as well as to the other arms.

30. E) The CAVALRY holds itself ready to enter the battle as soon as the infantry can advance without encountering any continuous obstacle.

As soon as it has succeeded in passing before the infantry, it maneuvers and acts with a view to widening the debouch, to masking or destroying the localized points of resistance and to gaining ground to carry out its mission.

When circumstances become entirely favorable, it starts the pursuit.

It must not be sacrificed to the impatience of finding a use for it.

31. F) The OTHER ELEMENTS OF COMBAT OR VARIOUS MEANS are used in conformity with the special provisions specified by the command in his orders, notably :

32. Tanks. — It is the mission of the tanks to destroy the enemy's accessory defenses and to reduce his resistance by a close and immediate action. They constitute an armored artillery of accompaniment which acts close at hand and *in close liaison* with the assaulting infantry.

Their use must be considered, either for attacking by surprise on a front habitually calm, or, in an operation regularly organized, for accompanying the infantry at for prolonging a first success by attacking immediately the second line positions which may not have been previously destroyed by our artillery.

In the accomplishment of their mission the tanks will meet as their principal obstacle the fire of the hostile artillery. The condition of their success therefore is a very careful organization of counter-battery, served by a very vigorous aviation. For the same reason they must not be employed on a terrain dominated by terrestrial observation posts which it will be impossible to blind.

Finally, the action of tanks is useful only if it can be immediately exploited by the infantry for whose profit it is exercised. To obtain this result, it will always be well to execute before the attack rehearsals of combined maneuvers of the infantry and tanks.

The Various Large Units.

33. A) The DIVISION. — The lessons of the war have led the High Command to constitute, with the different arms, an elementary group capable of conducting an attack by its own means over a terrain in which the action of the commanders in all echelons can make itself felt in the necessary time.

It is the division : *the division is the unit of attack.*

To use and distribute the divisions judiciously, it is essential to determine the offensive possibilities of the infantry.

The base of the calculation is the battalion : *the battalion is the unit of combat.* Experience proves that, in an assault launched against organized positions, its combat front varies between 300 and 400 meters. Its capability for advance, which is especially a function of the importance of the organizations to be reduced, varies between 800 and 1200 meters. Having arrived at this limit, it must be possible also for the battalion to maintain itself and to organize.

In the division, the command defines the front of the battalions, the depth of their advance and, in case of need, fixes the lines where the successive battalions will pass the head battalions. This last operation is called the *passing of lines*.

The possibilities of the division in front and in depth depend on the number of battalions brought into line or echeloned in depth.

The *division in square formation* is a divisional formation of three regiments side by side, with three battalions in line and three lines of battalions in depth : the offensive possibility is thus about 1200 meters in front and 2000 to 3000 meters in depth, with passing of lines (*).

34. This formation can not be considered as exact, and these figures are given only as a suggestion.

In a general way a large unit must be assigned a front narrow in proportion to :

The distance of the objectives assigned.

The importance of the organizations to be reduced.

The favorable character of the terrain for the development of the success.

Inversely, it is possible to extend one's front when the objectives are limited in depth, without prospect of development, and when the organizations to be reduced are either unimportant or in a position to be seriously threatened by attacks directed against their flanks.

An excess in the offensive possibilities in front and in depth may also be allowed in case surprise is the main element of the preparation.

But, even in this case, the offensive possibilities of a large unit have a limit which one must be able to determine according to circumstances : a division engaged in the first line in an attack can not advance indefinitely, even if its losses are insignificant.

This fact must enter into the calculation of the command with regard to the engagement of second line or reserve divisions.

(*) It must be observed that the capacity for advance of a division having three successive lines of battalions can not be equal to three times the capacity for advance of a battalion : for the battalions which have to execute passing of lines can not, after this operation, be considered as fresh and capable of their maximum service.

A surprise action may necessitate more divisions in the second line than in the first.

35. B) The ARMY CORPS. — Aside from elements independent or attached, the army corps is a group composed normally of from two to four divisions.

The *army corps in square formation* is a formation of four divisions with two in the first line and two in the second, immediately behind the first.

Such a group makes it possible to meet all the requirements of the combat :

The fire reserves (cannon or machine guns) of the second line divisions may be employed, from the beginning, for the benefit of the first line divisions.

All the echelons of the second line command insure the permanence of their reconnaissance and hold themselves ready to assume the combat on their own account, either with a view to the continuation of the offensive or to launch or repulse counter-attacks.

Successive attacks may be developed very rapidly by the passing of second line divisions in front of first line divisions, and by their exchange of rôles. This operation is called an *passing* of divisions.

When an army corps comprises less than four divisions it will be well to engage it on a front where the advance to be achieved is slight in depth. In this case it will usually be formed by divisions side by side.

Square army corps are capable by their own means of an advance of several kilometers and possibly of an appreciable development of the success.

Their capacity will be the greater the more judiciously the succession of the efforts of the divisions has been arranged. It is usually well to combine the passings so that each time the leading division may have given the maximum of its offensive capacity without reaching the point of physical or moral exhaustion and without suffering too great losses. It may then, by dropping back, assume the rôle of the second line.

On the other hand, when a leading division has been held to the point of exhaustion, *there will be not an passing but a relief,* that is, this division must be withdrawn and sent to the rear to be reorganized, exchanging roles with a large unit in reserve.

36. C) The ARMY. — The army is composed of a variable number of army corps or of independent divisions and it has at its disposal moreover extensive means of all sorts.

It has large units *engaged* and others in *reserve.* The army commander must be able, with his reserves, to intervene in the course of the battle to develop the success and to meet the requirements of the reliefs.

The various echelons of the attack and the exercise of the command.

37. The distribution of the infantry among the large units includes *assaulting troops* and *reserve troops.*

38. A) ASSAULTING TROOPS usually include all the battalions which, in the first line divisions, are placed under the direct command of the brigade commanders or the divisional infantry commanders.

These battalions are divided into :
First line battalions.
Second line or supporting battalions.
Battalions at the disposal of the brigade commanders or the divisional infantry commanders.

It is essential that the brigade commander or the divisional infantry commander have units at his disposal in order to exercise a personal and immediate influence in the course of the development of the attack.

These various echelons insure the working of the passing *of lines* and will make it possible to ward off unforeseen attacks and to extend the first gains (*).

(*) This distribution of battalions is an initial distribution. As the action develops after the various passing of lines, all the battalions having been successively engaged, the brigade commanders or divisional infantry commanders have no longer, properly speaking, any available units. In fact, a battalion which has furnished its attack, and which has been passed by another, is still capable of a certain effort, of holding a trench, for example, against a counter-attack, but not of movements.

39. B) The RESERVE TROOPS are:

Either first line battalions of the infantry divisions which the infantry division commanders hold at their disposal.

Second line large units, which constitute the troops at the disposal of the commanders of the army corps engaged.

Or the reserve large units of the army or group of armies.

These reserve echelons are a means, for all the commanders of large units, to intervene personally in the combat and to insure the development of the success as soon as the chance offers.

They serve to aid the working of the change of lines, the passings and the *reliefs.*

40. C) The EXERCISE OF THE COMMAND is insured in all the echelons in conformity with the provisions of the plans of action and engagement. It must be facilitated by the measures provided in the plans of liaison.

41. In the first line infantry divisions and to the degree permitted by the provisions of the plan of liaison, the commanders of all the assaulting units and of the entire body of assaulting troops and the infantry division commanders establish themselves so as to see as well as possible the battle field and to exercise an immediate and constant control.

Before the departure, the command posts are found ordinarily :

For a first line battalion commander, near the parallel of departure.

For an infantry regiment commander or a divisional infantry commander (*), on a line with the units at their disposal.

For an infantry division commander, near his reserves.

It is indispensable that the preparatory works should have insured at each one of these command posts the proper functioning of liaisons of all sorts.

(*) All that is said in the present instruction concerning divisional infantry commanders applies equally to brigade commanders.

The infantry division commanders must have installed, with full equipment, an initial command post thus far advanced, in which the views are good, the telephonic communications are insured, the ways of approach practicable, sufficiently defiladed and allowing as much possible the approach of motor cars; where the shelters are spacious enough to accommodate also the divisional artillery commander and his staff, as well as, temporarily, the second line infantry division commander with part of his staff, his divisional infantry commanders and his divisional artillery commanders. It is very important that this command post should have views over the terrain beyond the base of departure (or be connected with a nearby observation post having such views), for it will be very difficult and very slow to move later.

In the course of the action and, preferably, during the time of halt between two consecutive attacks, the command posts of the assaulting troops are moved so as to be kept within reach of information and observation points. These displacements are provided for, organized, and as far as possible prepared so as to insure the proper functioning of the liaisons.

The displacement of the command posts of the infantry division commanders must be the object of detailed provisions from which will be derived, in the plan of liaisons, the prescriptions relative to the throwing forward of the telephonic and other liaisons and the temporary measures necessary to insure the permanence of the command during this displacement.

42. The **Army Corps Commanders** engaged choose and establish their command post according to principles analogous to those given above for the infantry division commanders of the first line.

In order to avoid bringing into action considerable effectives of workmen, it will usually be sufficient to arrange a command post connected with their Headquarters.

43. In the second line infantry divisions, all the unit

commanders must hold themselves ready to act rapidly, conformably to the arrangements provided by the plans of engagement or on the demand of the moment, and for this purpose they must keep themselves constantly informed on the preparation, the launching and the evolution of the attack.

The second line infantry division commander (with his divisional infantry and divisional artillery commanders) usually stays at the command post of the first line infantry division commander or in its immediate proximity, to follow the development of the action, to prepare and issue orders for all the maneuvers of passing of lines, or if necessary, for maneuvers of relief.

The divisional infantry, the infantry regiment and the battalion commanders remain in liaison with their superior commander and with the commanders of units that are advancing before them. They must not lose sight of the fact that they must be at the head of their units at the moment when the latter are to advance, and consequently they regulate all their displacements.

44. In reserve large units, the commanders of all echelons take the place assigned to them by the plan of action or engagement emanating from superior authority.

III. — METHOD TO BE PURSUED IN CASE THE ENEMY RETIRES.

45. The previsions pertaining to the use and distribution of forces and means for an offensive action must be completed by indicating the measures to be taken in case the enemy attempts to retire to intact lines chosen by him and thus baffle the attack.

In such a contingency, it will be necessary to change the assault formation to a march formation, open all the formations and bring up all the units and resources which can be used for reëstablishing communications.

A square army corps, engaged with a view to attacking

upon a narrow front (about 3 kilometers) can not usually send forward, upon such a front, more than one of its 4 divisions and this upon the following conditions :

That it echelon itself in depth.

That it make use of a road whose reëstablishment will be insured in proportion to its advance.

That it take along only an amount of artillery proportional to the quantity of ammunition that can be brought up.

And that it adapt the movement of its combat trains to the exigencies of the situation.

The main body of troops which are no longer used in the advance formation should be :

One part, detailed to reëstablish and police the communications.

A second part, kept in place.

A third part, reassembled in the rear.

CHAPTER III.

SPECIAL CONDITIONS FOR THE EMPLOYMENT OF THE ARTILLERY.

46. The artillery opens a passage for the infantry.

The general principles for its employment have been given in Chapter II.

It follows that the artillery has multiple missions upon the battle field requiring varied combinations in the use of its various materiel.

Consequently all the echelons of the command must pay special attention to giving its artillery *complete* and *precise* orders for execution and to superintending the execution of these orders in all the phases of the struggle.

I. — EMPLOYMENT.

47. The employment of the artillery is based upon the demand for :

Power, which will facilitate the attack (this power will

be obtained not only by bringing into action considerable materiel, but also by the *concentration* of these means upon the objectives attacked).

Depth, which will make it possible to give each attack the amplitude desired by the command.

Continuity, which permits rapidity in the succession of the attacks, thanks to an advance of the artillery combined with that of the infantry.

The conditions for its employment are regulated by the *plan of employment,* the main principles of which will be enumerated in the second part.

These plans refer to the employment of the artillery before the attack. In case the attempt at surprise is the primary element of the preparation, the use of the artillery before the attack may be reduced.

Determination of objectives and tactical use of the fires.

48. The knowledge of the objectives, which is the fundamental data for artillery action, is insured by the organs of information at the disposal of the command (intelligence section, aeronautic service, artillery intelligence service). These organs cooperate to maintain, each day, before and during the operations, a detailed plan of the batteries and organizations of the enemy.

A thorough examination of all the elements of information by the command and the artillery makes it possible to determine the principal objectives to be swept. Moreover the detailed reconnaissances of the terrain carried out with the commanders of the attacking units establishes accurately the various objectives for the artillery of destruction.

In the course of the operations, the search for information of any sort concerning the defensive organizations and batteries of the enemy, and the time by transmission of this information to the command and to the artillery is of main importance.

49. A) Batteries and terrestrial or aerial observation posts of the enemy.

The artillery must combat the enemy's artillery in order to destroy or efficiently neutralize it and direct its fire upon the observation posts to destroy or blind them. This struggle is pursued before, during and after the attack.

The counter-battery fires are insured at all times by the heavy long guns, high power artillery and heavy howitzers not assigned to the divisional groups.

The light artillery and heavy howitzers assigned to the infantry divisions also engage in these fires outside of the period designated for destructive fire against the enemy's defensive organizations.

The *destruction* of batteries is one of the certain guarantees of success : it must be among the principal cares of the command.

Neutralization, particularly neutralization by special shells, completes the destructions which are considered insufficient and takes the place of those which it has been impossible to effect. It will hence be used to a great extent for silencing batteries incompletely demolished and those which may have escaped the destruction fires.

50. The artillery must at the same time aid the aeronautic service and the various organs of the anti-aircraft defense in policing the air : this is the object of the fires *against the balloons and avions.*

The command must provide them by assuring a close liaison between the anti-aircraft defense, the attacking large units and the different echelons of the aviation.

51. B) Defensive organizations of the enemy.

It is necessary :

To open passages through the obstacles that obstruct the advance of our infantry and to destroy the principal organs of the defense.

To take away all combative energy from the defenders, by the demoralizing effects which well regulated fire produces, either rapid and short, or slow and prolonged.

The *destruction fires* are maintained by the light artillery, the trench artillery, the heavy howitzers, and the high power artillery and in exceptional cases by the heavy long guns.

The command determines the precise objectives to be swept. The trenches and wire entanglements need not be entirely destroyed, but the necessary openings must be made and the important points crushed. In the same manner a whole village or woods should not be fired upon, but only certain clearly defined parts of them : those which it is necessary to attack or which flank the objectives to be attained.

The *control of the work of destruction is indispensable.* It is important that no infantry attack be launched before the necessary breaches have been made.

When the destruction of the entanglements thus controlled are insufficient, the infantry division commander reports to the army corps commander and requests extra time and means for achieving them.

As to the other organizations, the important parts must be destroyed, but it is vain to attempt to demolish them completely; the infantry division commander supplies this need by neutralization fires and by a *procedure of attack* thanks to which the enemy may be *surprised and caught* in his works or dugouts.

52. C) COMMUNICATIONS AND ESTABLISHMENTS OF THE ENEMY.

In order to increase the discomfiture of the opponent, by preventing the arrival of reinforcements, or reliefs and supplies of all kinds, the artillery must also sweep, in the rear of the front attacked, the reassembling places, the establishments (*) and the communications of the enemy.

These fires are executed by guns of all calibres. They are called *harassing or prohibitive fires.*

The necessary information is furnished by the study of photographs and questioning prisoners.

(*) Besides, certain establishments (particularly stations and ammunition depots) will be the object of destruction fire generally devolving upon the high power artillery.

Each terrestrial or aerial observer who discovers an important objective, and particularly moving or assembling troops, must immediately notify the batteries with which he is in communication; it is the duty of the latter to use or have this information used.

53. D) ELEMENTS OF THE ENEMY'S COUNTER-OFFENSIVE OR COUNTER-ATTACK.

An offensive action in preparation or in the course of execution occasionally encounters attacks which the enemy undertakes either as a prohibitive measure or as a reprisal.

It is the task of the artillery first to break up the enemy's preparations of attack, afterwards to check his attacks if they are launched.

The artillery must reply to any preparation of attack against our position by counter-preparation fire which consists in :

Opening fire upon the enemy's artillery with the counter-batteries in order to neutralize or destroy them.

Opening fire with all the destructive artillery upon the first trenches and the organized positions of the enemy, *concentrating* the fires immediately beyond the threatened zone.

Sweeping the lines of communication and establishments in the sector concerned.

If in spite of the counter-preparation the enemy's attack succeeds in debouching, the artillery launches its *barrage fires.*

54. E) ELEMENTS FORMING THE ACTIVE DEFENSE OF THE ENEMY'S ORGANIZATIONS.

The hostile infantry, after having taken refuge underground from the destructive fires, will rush from the dugouts to oppose the advance of the attacking infantry if it is not held under fire; the attacking infantry must therefore continue to receive the immediate, accurate and powerful support of its artillery during the entire advance, under penalty of being stopped by the fires of the defense, particularly by those of the machine guns.

This is the object of the *accompanying and protective fires*.

55. The *accompanying fires* are for the purpose of directly supporting the infantry attack by preventing defenders of the zone attacked from manning the trenches or approach trenches and installing machine guns in any point of the terrain whatsoever (open fields, shell holes, etc...), and by forming a mask behind which the infantry will be able to advance *by pressing close behind the shells*.

They consist of :

1) *Creeping barrages* with explosive percussion shells by the light artillery, in variable cadence, moving at the rate of advance fixed by the command for the infantry (this rate must be regulated for the different stages of the attack according to the form or condition of the terrain and its concealment from the enemy).

2) *Raking fire*, with time shells by the light artillery, intended to reach the occupants of shell holes. The shortest limit of this fire corresponds to the farthest limit of the creeping barrage.

The accompanying fires are fixed immediately beyond each of the intermediate objectives where the infantry must halt in order to allow its units to come up and to reform

They resume their advance either at a fixed hour or at this hour altered under the conditions explained in paragraph 194, or upon the demand of the infantry; then establish themselves immediately beyond the normal objective to permit the infantry to install itself there.

Under any circumstances and at every minute during the attack they insure to the infantry, wherever it may be, the direct support which must never cease.

Beyond the normal objective, the command may order the accompanying fire to form caging fire, to permit the infantry detachments to carry out reconnaissances or raids upon the enemy's batteries. After executing these reconnaissances or raids, these fires will eithe· again be directed beyond the normal objective, or they will accompany the infantry in its advance towards the possible objective.

56. The *protective fires* are fires upon determ'ned objectives, which extend beyond the accompanying fires. Their purpose is :

To blind all points from which the assaulting waves can be seen.

To neutralize the flankings.   ·

To isolate the zone attacked by prohibitive fires upon all the immediate approaches (trenches, approach trenches) and those more distant (passages, trails, roads).

To systematically sweep the probable reassembling zones of the enemy and to catch instantly any counter-attacks by the enemy under a rapid fire.

To maintain during and after the operation, as long as the command judges necessary, a protective barrage upon the flanks of the attack and assist, during this period, the batteries of accompaniment in covering the attacking front.

They are executed by the light artillery batteries not detailed for accompanying fire and by the heavy howitzers.

They usually consist in frontal, oblique and enfilade fires which move by jumps of variable distances. They are lifted at the moment when they are joined by the creeping barrage and are directed upon the following objectives.

It is necessary to be very careful in the use of oblique and enfilade fires and to be certain that they do not imperil the advance of the neighboring units.

The protective fires are of particular importance from the time the infantry reaches the normal objective, to protect it, in cooperation with the accompanying fire, against counter-attacks and counter-offensive. But the displacement of the light artillery also begins at this time; it will therefore be necessary to use for protective fire, in conjunction with the batteries of light artillery which remain in position (batteries of accompaniment), the heavy long guns in order to conceal the above mentioned displacements and to remedy the loss in the intensity of fire, resulting from these. This use will be more justified and possible as the enemy's artillery becomes more completely disorganized.

57. When the infantry has reached the normal objective, the procedure for accompanying and protective fire must be modified as prearranged and according to circumstances.

In particular, the accompanying fire is transformed to a barrage adapted to the position effectively occupied.

The plans of counter-preparation prepared in advance must be adapted to the situation.

Barrage and counter-preparation must be permanently insured by making allowances for the displacements effected by the artillery.

58. The accompanying and protective fire require a *close liaison* between the infantry and the artillery.

But, whatever groups or battalions may be assigned to support the regiments or battalions, these groups or battalions always remain under the orders of the infantry division commander, who, by means of the divisional artillery commander centralizes the command of the whole of the infantry division artillery.

59. The army corps commander will be able, if occasion arise, to reinforce the divisional artillery in the accomplishment of any of these missions, by calling upon certain batteries ordinarily employed in counter-battery fire.

However, this measure, which will only constitute a momentary support, must not weaken the counter-battery action.

Choice of emplacement.

60. The emplacement of a battery is essentially a function of its mission. The various artillery (counter-battery and destruction artillery) and the various materiel

composing them must therefore receive emplacements from which they will be able to fulfil most efficiently and most economically the mission assigned to them.

61. A) DISTRIBUTION OF EMPLACEMENTS IN THE DIRECTION OF THE FRONT.

Except for the artillery of accompaniment which fires in the axis of the attack, the endeavor to produce a large proportion of oblique and enfilade fires leads to a choice of emplacements which may be independent, to a certain degree, especially for the heavy artillery, of the formation of the large units.

The command should not allow itself to be checked by the material difficulties arising from such an arrangement : the solution of this difficulty is especially a question of system and organization.

62. B) ECHELONNEMENT IN DEPTH OF THE EMPLACEMENTS.

The artillery is whenever possible pushed far forward so that it will be able to :

Counter-sweep the batteries which the enemy tends to remove farther and farther.

Carry out the destruction, harassing, prohibitive and accompanying fire upon as deep a zone as possible.

Reduce to the minimum the changes of position which tend to retard and weaken the action.

However, it is necessary to take into account :

a) Special qualities of the various materiel and ammunition in order to sweep advantageously the first position.

b) Form of terrain, in order to insure the batteries the minimum defilading without which they might be unable to fulfil their mission;

c) The necessity of avoiding crowding too many batteries upon a small area where they might be simultaneously neutralized by a small number of hostile batteries or by gas attacks.

d) The necessity of insuring counter preparation.

In short, the artillery will be pushed as far forward as possible, but will preserve a certain echelonnement in depth adapted to its mission, to the characteristics of the materiel and to the terrain.

Aerial observation. — Terrestrial observation.

63. Artillery fire is efficient only when it can be accurately controlled.

Accurate fire control requires a very complete organization of the observation : *this condition is essential to the efficient use of artillery.*

Observation includes aerial and terrestrial observation.

64. The conditions for the organization and employment of *aerial observation* are fixed by special rules. In spite of the greater and greater efficiency of this method of observation, it can not fulfil all the needs of the artillery. Also it is greatly influenced by atmospheric conditions :

Hence the necessity for organizing terrestrial observation with the greatest care.

65. *Terrestrial observation* utilizes three kinds of observation posts :

a) *Information observation posts* managed by the terrestrial observation section of intelligence research, used for finding and watching objectives, for ranging and controlling certain fires;

b) *Observation posts of the artillery command,* permitting the direction and control of the work of the batteries.

c) *Observation posts for ranging and firing,* reserved for battalions and batteries.

Before the attack, the organization of the observation includes :

A detailed reconnaissance of the terrain and works of installation.

The establishment of communications connected with the artillery system.

The centralization of information concerning each observation post and its transmission to the units concerned stationed in the sector and in neighboring sectors.

66. In the course of the advance, the artillery battalions throw out reconnaissances to look for new observation posts on the conquered terrain. These reconnaissances are directed by the troops of attacking infantry and the liaison detachments.

The artillery has the new observation posts occupied as soon as possible, installs the communications and seeks to improve its means of observation rapidly by more detailed reconnaissances.

II. — DISTRIBUTION AND COMMAND.

67. The distribution of artillery to the attacking units is influenced by :

The study of the front to be attacked.

The characteristics of the different materiel.

The time that the command wishes to devote to artillery preparation.

The distribution fixed by the command serves as a base for the effective execution of the works and the arrangements for the artillery of the infantry divisions and the army corps, as well as for the provisions for ammunition supply. These works or arrangements and these provisions, with the installations that they involve, must necessarily be made in the sectors comprised in the zone of the general attack as well as in the sectors more or less close to this zone designated by the command.

Assignments to large units.

68. The distribution of artillery and the organization of the command are based on the following principles :

1) All artillery put at the disposal of an echelon of

command (infantry division, army corps, army) is grouped under the orders of a single commander.

2) The calibres are distributed among the echelons, leaving to each echelon the batteries which normally work for it, and grouping in the superior echelon those that have a normal action over several sectors.

3) The rapid intervention of the greatest possible number of batteries for the benefit of the troops that need them is prepared in all degrees (concentrations, etc...).

69. *To the attacking infantry divisions* is assigned the artillery (light artillery, heavy howitzers, trench artillery) corresponding to their mission; in each divisional sector, this artillery must be placed entirely under the orders of the infantry division commander.

When the infantry divisions of an army corps succeed each other in the sector, the army corps commander fixes the conditions of relief of the divisional artilleries and their commanders, so as to insure the continuity of artillery action in the best possible manner.

70. *To the army corps* are assigned :

The counter-battery artillery necessary to attack the hostile batteries placed in the army corps's zone of action.

Some howitzers or mortars from the high power heavy artillery destined to work for several infantry divisions : these are put at the disposal of the infantry divisions for very definite missions.

All this artillery remains under the orders of the army corps commander.

71. *To the army* are assigned the fractions of heavy artillery, of long range heavy or high power heavy artillery necessary for the special missions which concern the sectors of several army corps and to attack methodically the enemy's heavy artillery which is out of the zone of action of the army corps counter-battery artillery.

This artillery is under the orders of the army commander; he may put it, wholly or in part, for a definite mission or a

definite time, at the disposal of an army corps commander

72. VARIOUS GROUPS. — In an army corps sector of
attack :

a) The **divisional artillery** includes a variable number of
battalions or batteries of light artillery, heavy howitzers
and trench artillery.

In order to facilitate the rapid transmission of orders and
the superintendance of their execution, the divisional
artillery commander organizes *groups*, considering :

The missions to be fulfilled.

The liaisons to be insured between the artillery and the
infantry.

The organic cohesion of artillery to be respected.

These groups may be, according to circumstances :

Either *homogeneous*, that is, constitued of a single materiel.

Or *mixed*, that is, including various materiel.

Each group commander, while insuring his mission and
his liaison with the infantry, remains under the orders of
the infantry division commander, by the intermediary of
the divisional artillery commander.

b) The **counter-battery artillery** is under the direct
orders of the artillery commander of the army corps,
who organizes it also into groups; each group ordinarily
has as normal zone of action the sector assigned to one
infantry division.

The artillery commander of the army corps organizes
the command by utilizing the heavy artillery staffs at his
disposal, respecting as far as possible the existing organization of officers. He may either attach the heavy artillery commander of the army corps to himself or confide
to him the command of a group.

Zones of action.

73. It is necessary :

On the one hand, to insure the immediate opening of fire upon the objectives marked by the observation, avoiding the confusion resulting from the superposition of fires on the same objective.

On the other hand, to reserve the means of accomplishing oblique and enfilade fire or concentration.

To this end the zones of action are divided into normal zones of action and possible zones of action.

74. The *normal zone of action* of the army corps is divided among the artillery commands of the army corps.

The normal zone of action of each infantry division corresponds ordinarily to the front of this infantry division and is limited in depth by a line corresponding to the objectives the attack on which the infantry division artillery can prepare and the defense of which it can support after they have been taken; it is fixed by the army corps.

The normal zone of action of the army corps artillery extends over all the zone of action of the army corps, beyond the limit above cited; it is fixed by the army within the limit of efficacious range of the pieces assigned to the army corps.

The normal zone of action of the army heavy artillery extends over all the zone beyond the preceding limit and up to the limit of the range of the pieces assigned to the army.

The normal zone of action of these commands is distributed among the groups or battalions, each one of which has thus a normal zone of action.

75. With a view to permitting reciprocal support and concentration, each group or battalion has *possible zones of action,* extended as widely as possible in the zone of its command and the contiguous zones.

The normal zones do not overlap, they are defined by very definite lines of the terrain or by alignments easy to note by the observers; the possible zones are common to several groups or battalions. Thus each objective is in the normal zone of a single group or battalion, and in the possible zone of several groups.

Fire in the normal zone of action of the group or battalion will be opened by order of the group or battalion commander. The rapid opening of a fire called for by avion or balloon will thus be insured.

On the other hand, fire upon an objective in the possible zone will be opened only on the demand or after the warning of the group or battalion commander in whose normal zone the objective is and who can not satisfy the demands of the observer.

Thanks to this arrangement, there should not be produced on a single objective, save in case of concentration fire, superpositions of fire rendering ranging impossible.

The zones of action and the corresponding groups must be very well known to the avion observers.

Sometimes, certain pieces or batteries are reserved to fulfil the demands for fire on fugitive objectives, made by avions. In this case, these pieces have as their normal zone the entire extent that they are capable of sweeping.

The distribution of the artillery in groups and the assignment to these groups of normal and possible zones of action give great flexibility to the artillery by permitting the *immediate opening of fire* upon any objective designated, as well as the *concentration of fire*.

Liaisons.

76. The timely intervention of the artillery requires completely and methodically organized liaisons in the interior of the groups and between the various command posts of the artillery.

These liaisons are insured by a double telephone system and if possible, by visual signalling.

Moreover, the artillery commanders (Army, Army Corps, Divisional Artillery, Heavy Artillery) must keep themselves posted, by liaison missions intrusted to officers of their staff, upon the situation, the work and the needs of the groups or battalions placed under their orders or operating in their neighborhood, and of the infantry which they support.

The liaisons between the artillery and the infantry are established in conformity with the *instruction upon liaison;* it is necessary to maintain a liaison between the counter-battery artillery and the infantry.

Artillery reinforcements.

77. It is often advantageous to place, in the rear of the fronts of attack, artillery available to the commands :

Either to bring fresh batteries into action;

Or to insure the relief of the artillery which the duration of the action renders necessary.

III. — POSSIBILITIES OF MANEUVERING ARTILLERY AND ITS DISPLACEMENTS.

78. It is necessary to *maneuver* the artillery, during an entire offensive action, and to insure the continuity of its action for the benefit of the infantry by following the advance of the infantry.

Its displacements are affected *by echelons,* when possible during a halt between two successive attacks, and with the greatest possible rapidity.

The plan of displacement of the artillery, which is directly connected with the plan of communications and plan of liaisons, provides for each echelon of the command (army, army corps, infantry division) the detailed measures concerning these movements.

The emplacements to be occupied in the course of the action are either in front or in the rear of the parallels of departure.

79. *a)* The emplacements situated in the rear of the parallels of departure must be prepared before the engagement and improved as soon as the infantry has achievep the necessary advance (topographic preparation of fire, dugouts for the personnel and ammunition, bringing up a first supply, telephonic communications, etc.); they can then be occupied very quickly.

A certain number of them may even be partly or wholly equipped in advance, with the understanding that the batteries will not reveal themselves until the favorable moment.

These works will be concealed and camouflaged with the greatest care. It will be well if they can be carried out by day.

80. *b*) The emplacements to be established in the enemy's zones are studied in detail from maps, aerial photographs, reconnaissances from the terrestrial observation posts, etc. The materiel necessary for rapid and summary installation is prepared in advance (*). Working parties detailed for the construction of batteries and placed at the disposal of the artillery are united under the orders of artillery officers.

As soon as the infantry has advanced, these emplacements are indicated upon the terrain and the working parties arrange them.

The command takes care at the same time to supply them as soon as possible with the communications which have been arranged for.

IV. — REPLENISHING OF AMMUNITION.

81. It is necessary to endeavor, in the calculations relative to the replenishing, to organize the *daily bringing up of one day's* supply, as defined in supplement no. 1 (Table X): the tonnage is considerable (**).

The supplies which may be accumulated in advance near the pieces must be considered only as a margin : on

---

(*) It is particularly necessary :

1) To prepare a second set of platforms for all the materiel which require their use.

2) To provide camouflage arrangements adapted for terrain whose occupation is under consideration.

(**) It has occasionally reached 2000 tons for an army corps having two infantry divisions engaged, without counting the trench artillery or high power artillery.

one hand to provide for the advance of the artillery and on the other to diminish the chances of damage by the weather and the enemy's fire, it is necessary that these supplies should not be too numerous.

82. In the army corps the direction of the replenishment of ammunition devolves upon the corps artillery commander.

With a view to obtaining the maximum efficiency from all the means placed in operation to insure the replenishment of the ammunition (artillery munition train, horse drawn or motor trucks, first line of wagons and light columns, auxiliary division train or division train, park sections, 60 centimeter track) the whole of this service is centralized in the army corps by the commander of the corps artillery park, both for the replenishment of ammunition of the army corps, of the heavy artillery or the trench artillery, and for the guarding and management of the munition depots allotted to the army corps.

Normally the commander of the corps artillery park has at his disposal the divisional artillery park and the corps artillery park; but these organs are not sufficiently supplied to transport daily to a distance the quantity of artillery munitions necessary; it is advisable therefore to facilitate this task :

1) **For the light artillery.** — a) By reducing the distance for horse drawn conveyances by installing advanced depots or distribution points where the munitions will arrive by camion or by 60 centimeter railroad.

b) By reinforcing them with conveyances loaned by the army (park sections, auxiliary division train) or drawn from the resources of the army corps (division train).

The first line of battery wagons cooperates in supplying munitions as far as indicated by the commander of the corps artillery.

2) **For the heavy artillery.** — a) By using the 60 centimeter railroad (recommended especially for large calibres) (*).

(*) When there is not a complete sytem 60 centimeter track serving the

b) By using the conveyances of the artillery munition train, horse drawn conveyances or motor trucks, first line of battery wagons, light columns, park sections, etc.

These means are wholly or partially united under the orders of the commander of the corps artillery park to which are joined some officers of the heavy artillery and who assure the most efficient service by the various conveyances (auto trucks for long trips by road, horse drawn conveyances for crossing fields).

3) **For the trench artillery.** — By conveying the munitions for the trench artillery as near the batteries as possible over the 40 or 60 centimeter tracks; they are then carried up to the guns by the means arranged by the batteries assisted by the auxiliaries.

83. Ammunition depots (*). — The choice of emplacements and the arrangement of ammunition depots, intermediate depots, etc., have considerable influence upon the efficiency of the replenishment of ammunition.

The depots must :

a) Have a competent command and the necessary workmen at their disposal (about one workman per ton of ammunition entering the depot each day, independent of the artillerymen detailed for its installation).

b) Be served by the 60 centimeter track, accessible at all times by camions and so arranged as to avoid congestion.

c) Permit simultaneous operation (unloading ammunition arriving from the rear, loading materiel to be evacuated, distribution of ammunition to the advanced units); which necessitates laying out independant ammunition platforms, paths and circuits.

d) Not be at the mercy of a terrestrial or aerial bom-

---

batteries it is very advantageous to arrange at least blocks of 40 or 60 centimeter tracks and small trucks intended to join the batteries to the nearest roads : thus the most difficult part of the transportation is avoided as well as the creation of very visible trails which betray the presence of the best camouflaged batteries.

(*) See Instruction on Ammunition under date of June 6th, 1917.

bardment and must be arranged in such a manner as to localize their effects.

e) Not be too far in the rear of the batteries to be served in order to insure the timely flow of ammunition toward the front.

Numerous services being interested in the proper functioning of the depots, their emplacement is fixed by the army which should usually take charge of the first installation and provide the necessary materiel.

84. Organs of replenishment for the batteries. — These organs of replenishment are very vulnerable. It is necessary to avoid grouping them and they should not be placed within the range of the enemy's medium range artillery. Their distance from the batteries is of little importance if they are well connected with these batteries.

CHAPTER IV.

SPECIAL CONDITIONS FOR THE EMPLOYMENT OF THE AERONAUTIC SERVICE.

85. The possibilities and the efficiency of the aeronautic service are influenced by two essential conditions :

The fighting power of the enemy's aviation, compared with our own.

The atmospheric conditions.

Aerial superiority is the primary condition in the work of the aeronautic service; it is indispensable to the success of the operations. It should be the primary consideration from the beginning to the end of the battle. Its elements are :

Superiority of means in number, in spirit of the personnel and in quality of the materiel.

In the proper employment of these means.

The aid furnished by the other arms (notably the artillery and machine guns).

I. — EMPLOYMENT.

86. The various missions of the aeronautic service have been taken up in chapter II. They are classified into :

Offensive missions.

Missions of observation and liaison.

This distribution of missions is not inflexible. Every avion may be called upon to fight and to observe.

Offensive missions.

87. A) Combat against the enemy's aeronautic service.

The purpose of this combat is :

To destroy the hostile aeronautic service.

To permit our aeronautic service to work in safety and to render hostile observation impossible or very difficult.

This combat comprises :

a) Attacks on hostile avions by combat groups operating singly or in liaison with the day bombardment groups.

b) Attacks on balloons.

c) Attacks on aviation grounds.

This combat is closely related to that of the terrestrial and anti-aircraft artillery from the point of view of mutual support and of communicating information.

It is also related to the aerial combat on parts of the front where the enemy's combat aviation will be retained or attracted by day bombing raids.

a) The **attacks on hostile avions** devolve on combat groups operating as offensive patrols. Day bombing raids executed in liaison with the combat groups may bring forth the hostile avions.

b) The **attacks on balloons** are performed by fast avions with incendiary devices :

In the form of a general operation to destroy the enemy's observation at a given moment (such as the moment of attack);

In the form of several isolated surprise attacks for the purpose of moral effect on the hostile pilots and to keep them far from the lines and at a low height.

c) The **attacks on the aviation grounds** are in the form of day and night bombardments.

The results of the combat against the enemy's aeronautics should be determined by the intelligence services (staff and aeronautic intelligence service).

Information is obtained from :

The study of the daily activity of the enemy's aeronautic service by observation from avions, balloons, by the anti-aircraft defense, by the radiogonometric posts, and by the troops.

The study of the movements of squadrons, especially by photographic and visual reconnaissances of aviation grounds.

The determination of the enemy's losses from reports of aviators, of the anti-aircraft defense, of troops and from the questioning of aviators taken prisoners, etc.

88. B) Bombardment.

Bombing raids by avions cause important material results and a strong moral effect.

Bombing raids should be organized methodically. The action includes :

The knowledge of the objectives.

The choice of objectives.

The execution.

a) The **knowledge of the objectives** comes under the intelligence service (staff and aeronautic services of the group of armies and the army).

It results in the execution of maps, lists of objectives, large scale maps, and photographs of each objective when possible.

b) The **choice of objectives** is made by the command after considering :

Their value, which depends on their nature but may also vary with the plans of the command and the phases of combat.

Their vulnerability. Bombing raids by avions are not very accurate and serious effects can only be obtained against large and vulnerable objectives. Bombing raids on batteries and railway lines, except stations and important depots, will usually be without results. Bombing raids on such objectives and on objectives covered by our artillery are carried out only for their moral effect.

During an offensive action the most vital objectives are the enemy's supply organs, especially those of the artillery, the aviation grounds, stations, billets, camps.

c) **Execution of bombardments.** — *Night bombing raids* permit throwing a relatively large number of projectiles with fairly good accuracy if the crews are skilled.

Day bombing raids are usually less effective but, in addition to their use against hostile aviation, they permit immediate control of the fire and observation of results (photographs).

89. C) INTERVENTION IN THE INFANTRY COMBAT.

This intervention gives great material results and has a very great moral effect on the enemy and on our own troops.

The attacks are executed in fast avions by machine guns (possibly by bombs, grenades, darts) by the .

Army Corps aviation on the near objectives (troops in trenches, nests of resistance);

Army aviation, the combat groups and the bombing groups on the distant objectives (reserve batteries, troops on the march, trains).

Missions of observation and liaison.

90. AERIAL OBSERVATION.

a) **Avions.** — Avions enable rapid, accurate, and vertical observation of the most distant points. Photographs can be taken.

They can send simple messages by wireless and receive them by panels.

A large personnel is necessary to insure the permanency of avion observation.

91. The efficiency of avion observation depends on the security of the machine and occupants.

The combat avions and the anti-aircraft artillery should provide a zone of relative security where the observation avions may operate alone.

Outside of this zone, whose limits are not absolute and will almost completely disappear during a combat of movement, the safety of observation avions is insured by :

1º Their facilities of flight and their own armament.

2º Working in groups, especially at times and in zones where our combat avions are operating.

3º At times an immediate protection by combat avions.

Counter-battery fire by our artillery on the hostile anti-aircraft artillery and machine guns aids the action of the observation avions and the combat avions.

92. *b*) **Balloons.** — Balloons can not rise above 2000 meters. Their working altitude is usually between 1000 and 1500 meters.

Because of their vulnerability they must be kept far from the lines.

Their operation is almost entirely dependent on atmospheric conditions and parts of the terrain are defiladed from their view. On the other hand, it allowe the permanence of observation and keeps a constant telephonic liaison with the command.

Unless hindered by obstacles (bridges, trees, telegraph lines) they can be moved in inflated position on the ground or in the air.

Their security is insured by all the anti-aircraft materiel, by their own anti-aircraft machine gun sections, and to a small degree, by the armament carried in the balloon car.

93. Missions of observation and liaison include :

Missions of intelligence.

Missions of fire.

Missions of command.

Missions of liaison.

94. A) MISSIONS OF INTELLIGENCE.

Distant reconnaissances follow the installations and movements of the enemy in the rear zone.

In the war of positions it is very seldom that the movements of the enemy corresponding, for example, to a reinforcement (movements of trains or colums of troops) will be conclusively determined directly from observation. The intentions of the enemy are usually deduced from a study of the modifications of his defense lines, of the railways, stations, camps and aviation grounds. Photographs are essential for this study.

The distant reconnaissances are ordinarily executed by the army squadrons at a high altitude, by fast avions supplied with cameras and accompanied when necessary by combat avions.

Close reconnaissances follow the enemy's defensive organization and his artillery situation.

They include :

The execution of photographic or visual reconnaissances (the former are very necessary in a war of positions).

The constant observation of the terrain during all missions. (Balloons are best suited for permanent observation which deals mostly with the discovery of gun flashes from batteries in action).

Close reconnaissances are usually executed by the army corps aeronautic service (avions and balloons).

The use of fast or heavily armed avions (three-seaters) is especially advantageous for photographic missions.

95.   B) MISSIONS OF FIRE (ranging, control, observation).

These missions are executed as indicated by the *Instruction on aerial observation in liaison with the artillery.*

96.   C) MISSIONS OF COMMAND.

These missions of command permit or facilitate :

1) The **maneuver** by insuring :
The knoweldge of the situation of the enemy.
The knowledge of the situation of the friendly troops.
The transmission of orders in special cases.

2) The **control of the execution** by a knowledge of :
The position of the means.
The progress of the destructions.
The advance.
The situation at the end of the combat.
The execution of these missions varies with the phases of the engagement but is usually in the form of visual reconnaissances at a low altitude (at times photographic reconnaissances).

97.   D) MISSIONS OF LIAISON.

In combat these missions (especially the accompanying of the infantry) are executed as indicated in the *Instruction on liaison.*

98. The success of the missions of fire and liaison demands from the aeronautic service and from all the other arms :

1) A rigid application of the procedures of liaison.

2) A training that will make the execution of the liaison automatic.

3) A faith in and a knowledge of one another.

II. — DISTRIBUTION OF MEANS AND THE COMMAND.

Aeronautic service of the group of armies.

99. For an offensive action the *aerial means* at the disposal of a group of armies comprise :

Combat and bombing groups.

Army squadrons.

Army corps squadrons, squadrons of the heavy artillery and of the high power heavy artillery.

Balloons.

,The commander of the group of armies :

1) Distributes the aeronautic units among the large units of the group of armies according to the missions assigned them and the quantity of supplementary means at their disposal (especially artillery means) :

2) Assigns the missions of the aeronautic units that he retains under his immediate orders.

3) Insures close liaison between the army aeronautic service and the combat and bombing groups.

The field officer of the aeronautic service assigned to the staff of the group of armies follows the use of all the aeronautic means. He may exercise the direct command of the units not assigned to the armies.

Army aeronautic service.

100. The *aerial means* at the disposal of an army comprise :

One or several combat and bombing groups.

One or several army squadrons.

Army corps squadrons, squadrons of the heavy artillery and high power heavy artillery.

Balloons :

One meteorological station.

The army commander :

1) Distributes the aerial means, following the principles indicated by the commander of a group of armies without however dissociating organic units such as combat groups;

2) Supervises the use of the aeronautic means in the subordinate units.

3) Assigns the missions of the units that he retains under his immediate orders.

4) Insures close liaison between the army aeronautic service, army corps aeronautic services and aeronautic service of adjacent army corps.

He has under him the *commander of the army aeronautic service* for commanding the units that he retains under his immediate orders and for following the use of the aeronautic units assigned to various formations.

Army corps aeronautic service.

101. *The army corps aeronautic service* comprises :

1) One chief (officer of the aeronautic personnel) and aids : aviation officer, intelligence officer, aerostation officer, in command of the army corps aerostation.

2) Aviation and aerostation units (squadrons, balloon, **and** photographic unit).

The army corps commander distributes the aerial means among the divisions and the army corps artillery and assigns the missions to those units that he retains under his immediate orders.

For an army corps having two divisions in line adopt the following organization :

One squadron and one balloon (of the army corps) insure the general missions of the army corps (command, photographs) and assist in observation for the benefit of the divisions and the army corps artillery.

One squadron and one balloon (of the division) are assigned to each first line infantry division.

One or two squadrons and one or two balloons (of the heavy artillery) are assigned to the army corps artillery.

The commander of the army corps aeronautic service commands these units and coordinates their effort. As a rule he is stationed at the landing ground, where he can best exercise his command. He frequently visits the army corps command post.

PART II.

THE PREPARATION.

PART II.

PREPARATION.

CHAPTER V.

PLANS.

I. — GENERAL PLAN OF ACTION.

102. A) THE GENERAL PLAN OF ACTION OF THE GENERAL, COMMANDER-IN-CHIEF, which is communicated to the army by abstracts only, consists of a number of consecutive and combined operations, that will be executed according to its provisions for time and place.

It fixes the order of urgency.

It indicates the measures *for the offensive preparedness* of the fronts concerned.

It distributes to the Groups of Armies all the materiel and units of workmen necessary for this preparedness.

When he deems it expedient, the General Commander-in-Chief gives the *orders for offensive actions* which prescribe:

Individual offensive actions with limited objectives, the execution of which is closely related to the secret provisions of the general plan, or

Combined offensive actions, the mutual missions of each unit being clearly indicated.

These orders contain :

The mission of the groups of armies and armies.

The nature of the preparation.

The principal phases of the operation and the conditions of surprise to be sought for each of these.

The distribution of the forces and means.

The previsions for following up the success.

The procedure in case of a withdrawal by the enemy.

103. B) THE GENERAL PLAN OF ACTION OF THE GROUP OF ARMIES is similarly drawn up.

It indicates the measures for the *offensive preparedness* of each part of the interested front by a plan of operations :

1) **Forward works.** — a) Offensive organizations : parallels, assembling places; approach trenches (with a normal profile or reduced profile) (*).

b) Commanding organs : command posts, observation posts.

c) Increasing the number of artillery emplacements : reconnaissances, drawing up a map indicating battery positions.

d) Avion landing stations, parks.

e) Camps and shelters for the attacking troops.

f) Liaison (especially underground).

g) Communications (automobile routes roads, bridges, trails, 60 centimeter tracks).

h) Materiel and food depots.

i) Water supply.

j) Medical service.

k) Prison camps.

2) **Rear works.** — a) Improving the normal gauge railways (special tracks, junctions, double tracks, spur tracks, warehouse for artillery, engineer parks, and evacuation hospitals), so as to distribute the loading stations, supply stations, the heavy railroad artillery, the evacuating stations, etc... according to the density of the troops.

(*) The advantage of making these works beforehand, even if only with a reduced profile, comes from the fact that they will be visible to hostile observation long in advance and will attract less attention, when they are deepened. It will also be much easier to put more workmen to work when the conditions demand.

The Commander-in-Chief orders the above works after a study of the ground made as indicated by the *instruction on the general organization of communications for an offensive action.*

The purpose of this study is to determine the works to be built, the improvements necessary, and the order of urgency of these works.

b) Extending the roads and tracks to communicate with the combat trains and the depots.

104. When the commander of a group of armies has received an *order for offensive action,* he draws up an order giving more detailed previsions.

This order fixes :

The mission of the armies.

The nature of the preparation.

The principal phases of the operation and the conditions of surprise for each of these.

The distribution of the forces and means.

The previsions for following up the success.

The procedure in case the enemy withdraws.

It also orders the works for an offensive preparedness.

II. — ARMY PLAN OF ACTION.

105. Usually the army will have been at the theater of operations a long time in advance. The commander and his staff will know the ground. They will have already contributed to the study of the project and the realization of the preparatory works for the offensive. They will only be called upon to perfect *their reconnaissance of the terrain and the study of the hostile organizations* by special aerial or terrestrial reconnaissances (photos, relief maps, information furnished by the intelligence sections of the staffs).

At times the operation will be entrusted to one army in formation or in reserve. In this case the commander and the staff of this army will first make the reconnaissances and studies which are indicated above and which constitute the fundamental data of the work.

The army plan of action deals with :

The large units in the sector concerning the works and the drawing up of the plans of engagement;

The large units designated for the attack concerning the final form and execution of these plans of engagement;

The artillery units, aeronautic units, and troops at the disposal of the army.

Outline of an army plan of actions.

106. The outline given below enumerates all the points which an army plan of action *may* include.

It does not follow that the plan *must* deal with all these points.

For each of these points the army plan of action provides for the units or organs immediately subordinate to the general in command of the army and does not deal with the details found in the plans drawn up by the smaller units.

Example : When the army plan of action includes a *plan of destruction*, a *plan of accompaniment of the attacks*, etc... it is for the purpose of enabling the commander of the army to assign the mission of each organ, and to give very general directions as to the use of all the forces and means, especially relating to the liaison between the elements immediately subordinate to him.

107. I. PURPOSE OF THE OFFENSIVE ACTION. — MISSION AND ZONE OF ACTION OF THE ARMY.

General conditions of the execution.

a) The scheme of maneuver.

b) Determination of the time for the preparation and for the execution of the attack.

c) The element of surprise.

108. II. DEFINING THE OBJECTIVES.

a) The objective of the offensive action : defined in front and depth.

b) Dividing the offensive action into several attacks : directions for the rapid succession of these attacks.

c) Assigning the objectives for the first attack :

Normal objective (also one or several intermediate objectives where the large units of the attack should halt and make sure of their liaison).
Possible objective.

d) Reconnaissance of the objectives for later attacks.

e) **General plan for the later attacks and for following up the success.**

109. III. GENERAL PLAN FOR USING THE ATTACKING TROOPS.

a) Density of the formations of attack at the various parts of the front and their distribution in depth.
Large units engaged (preferably in square formation).

b) Limits of the *zones of engagement* of the army corps (and when necessary, the *sectors of engagement* of the divisions of infantry in the first line not attached to an army corps).
Successive objectives for each army corps.
General directions for the *maneuvers of passing* at various stages.
Mission of the tactical units charged with covering the flanks of the army and with the liaison with adjacent armies.

c) Distribution of the forces and means at the disposal of the army.

Forces :

Infantry, artillery, aeronautic service, engineers, cavalry, tanks, flame projecting or Z companies, territorial troops, native troops, divisional machine gun companies, special detachments of workmen, liaison detachments.

Means .

Normal and narrow-gauge railways, automobile and wagon trains, ammunition and explosives, engineer materiel camouflage, material and tools for improving the communications, sanitary and administrative equipment.

d) Distribution of the forces and means held as an army reserve.

Mission of the Cavalry.

e) **Plan for bringing up the forces and means.**

Special arrangements for the infantry of the attacking troops during the preparation (reconnaissances, instruction, training).

Plan for bringing up the infantry.

f) Initial and subsequent positions of the command posts.

g) General precautions against gas.

h) General precautions against aerial bombardment.

110. IV. PLAN FOR USING THE ARTILLERY.

a) Organization of the command. — Groups.

Distribution of the missions between the army corps artillery and the army artillery.

Normal and possible zones of action.

Cooperation of the army corps with one another and with the army heavy artillery.

Observation.

Liaison.

b) Distribution of the emplacements.

Emplacements for the army artillery on the engagement ground of the various army corps.

Emplacements that the army corps should reserve for the army artillery or for the artillery of adjacent army corps.

Installation of the various materiel and groups and command posts of the army artillery.

c) Previsions for the first trial fires.

d) Installation and functioning of the meteorological service.

e) Plans for the period of destruction.

Plan for the destruction and neutralization of artillery : batteries, anti-aircraft batteries, observation posts, balloons, avions.

Plan for the destruction of the defensive organizations.

Plan for the harassing and prohibitive fire.

Plan for counter-preparation (prohibitive destructions, barrages, list of points of concentration).

Plan for false attacks by fire.

Use of machine guns for harassing and prohibitive fire — Fire to prevent the repair of the damage.

f) **Plan for accompanying and protecting the first attack :**

General directions.
Long range action by the army artillery.

g) **Plan of successive battery emplacements.**
Army batteries.
Procedure of shifting the batteries : relation between the plan of successive emplacements and the plan of communications.
Precautions for insuring the continuity of artillery fire while changing emplacements (especially the successive positions of the terrestrial observation sections of intelligence research and the sound ranging sections).

h) General directions for later attacks.

i) Ammunition supply :

General directions (sending supplies forward, during and after the attack, special shells).
Supplying the batteries of army artillery.

111. V. PLAN FOR USING THE TANKS.

a) Distribution and use of the tanks for destroying the defensive organizations.

b) Distribution and use of the tanks for accompanying the infantry.

112. VI. PLAN FOR USING THE ENGINEERS.

Distribution and mission of the engineer troops.

113. VII. PLAN FOR USING THE AERONAUTIC SERVICE

a) Distribution of the aeronautic materiel among the large units.

Allotment of missions to the army corps aeronautic service, to the army aeronautic service and to the aeronautic service of the group of armies.

Assigning landing stations, camps and ascending points for the balloons.

b) Bringing up the elements. Provisions for the first signs of activity.

c) Use before the attack.

Reconnaissance and photographs of the enemy's rear.

Destruction of the enemy's aviation and constructions by combat and bombardment.

Artillery ranging.

d) Use during the attack.

Combat and bombardment.

Reconnaissance and photographs of the rear.

Firing missions.

Later, the control of the infantry advance and the transmission of orders.

Advance of the balloons.

e) General provisions for the later attacks.

Plan for shifting the positions of the aeronautic service.

114. VIII. PLAN OF LIAISON.

a) The *various telephone systems,* completed, under construction, or under consideration (systems for the command, artillery, aeronautic service and anti-aircraft defense).

b) Assignment of individual technical characteristics to the *radio telegraphy posts* (length of wave, pitch, etc.) and the period assigned to each post for sending.

c) Organization of the *visual signaling.*

d) The code for liaison by *fireworks*.

e) Allotment of the *carrier-pigeons*.

f) Characteristic signs of *avions* and *balloons* on missions of liaison; conditions under which they may operate.

g) Assignment of *call letters* (indicatives).

h) The *liaison personnel* to be detached.

i) Indicating the centrals for the army telephone system, the lines of communication of the army corps, and the army corps intelligence centers.

j) Detaching units of workmen for extending the telephone system.

k) Materiel supply.

115. IX. PLAN OF INTELLIGENCE RESEARCH AND ITS DEVELOPMENT.

a) Special arrangements for hastening the transmission and use of information.

Have direct communication between the various organs (*) :

Infantry intelligence service.

Division and army corps intelligence service (Staff).

Division topographical service and army corps telegraph service.

Army corps and army artillery intelligence services.

Army corps and army aeronautic information service.

Photographic section.

Army topographical sections.

b) Subsequent detailing of certain organs of the army artillery intelligence service to the army corps artillery intelligence service :

From the terrestrial observation intelligence service :

From the sound ranging service.

c) Duties of the intelligence sections (Staff).

Instructions to the intelligence research organs.

Instructions on the questioning of prisoners.

(*) These direct communications should never do away with the regular communications prescribed by « The instruction on intelligence research ».

Special instructions to the army corps topographical section and the army topographical sections.

Instructions on the daily conferences between the representatives of the various research organs.

Centralization and use of information.

Drawing up of publications :

Maps to be made and kept to date. (Instruction on battle maps, maps, and special diagrams).

116. X. PLAN OF COMMUNICATIONS, SUPPLY AND EVACUATIONS.

A) **Communications.**

a) Use of railroads, (normal, metric, 60 centimeter).

b) Use of roads (reserved roads, one way traffic).

c) Automobile routes.

d) Policing the roads, bridges, paths, and the rear of the battlefield. Cleaning up the rear of the battlefield.

e) Duties of the provost with respect to communications and military police.

B) **Supply.**

a) Assigning the stations

b) Artillery service :

Warehouses . . . . . { site and organization,
Ammunition depots . { amount of supplies.

Assigning auto trucks and wagons for transport.

c) Engineer service.

Warehouses . . . . . { site and organization,
Depots . . . . { amount of supplies.

Assigning auto trucks and wagons for transport.

d) Administrative service :

Food . . . . { site and organization,
Water . . . . { amount of supplies.

Assigning auto trucks and wagons for transport.

e) Medical service .

Materiel depots . . . $\left\{ \begin{array}{l} \text{site and organization,} \\ \text{amount of supplies.} \end{array} \right.$

C) **Evacuations.**

a) Assignment of ambulances, hospitals and evacuation hospitals.

b) Detailed directions for the evacuations.

D) **Prisoners.**

Movement and formation of trains of prisoners.

E) **Directions for the advance.**

a) Railways and roads to be improved.

b) Assigning working units and the use of auto trucks and wagons for transport.

c) Supply of materiel for advancing the warehouses and depots.

117. XI. PLAN OF THE WORKS.

a) Arrangements for terminating or completing the *forward works* of the offensive preparation.

Offensive organizations.

Organs of command (command posts and observation posts).

Artillery emplacements.

Landing stations, aviation parks and auxiliary grounds

Depots and supply stations.

Camps and shelters.

Liaison.

Communications.

Water supply.

Medical service.

Prison camps.

b) Completion of the *rear works* (*).

---

(1) The rear works should be terminated at the moment an offensive action is ordered.   There should be left only a few works for the last moment.

c) Program of the *works after the attack,* conforming to the:
Plan of successive artillery positions.
Plan of successive aeronautic positions.
Plan of successive positions of command posts.
Plan of liaison.
Plan of advance of the communications and supplies.

d) Assigning the work places to the :

Troops in the sector when the plan was drawn up.
Attacking troops.
Special units of workmen (before, during and after the attack.

118. XII. PROCEDURE IN CASE OF AN ENEMY'S WITH-DRAWAL.

a) Recognizing an intended withdrawal.

b) Defining the zones of engagement of the large units (*) designated for the advance.

c) Indicating the lines of communication of the large units (**).

d) Directions for the first advance of the large units. Their support by the artillery not assigned to the advance and by the artillery of the assault.

e) Successive transversals at which the liaison between the large units of the advance should be insured.

f) Mission of the aeronautic service.
Reconnaissance of the enemy.
Reconnaissance of the first friendly lines.
Transmission of information and orders.
Assignment of mounted orderlies cyclists, and ground wireless posts to the aviation service.
Combat and bombardment.
Shifting of all or part of the aeronautic service and its rear organizations.

(*) It will be advantageous to retain as a point of departure the limits assigned to the army corps by the plan of action and to have them mark the limits of engagement of one infantry division in four.
(**) or the line of communication choose the route whose improvement is provided for in the zone of engagement of the large unit.

g) Mission of the engineers.

h) Mission of the cavalry (*).

i) Mission of labor detachments.

For improving roads and communications.

For advancing the materiel, ammunition and supplies.

For shifting the heavy artillery.

For extending the normal and narrow-gauge railways.

j) Extending the traffic facilities especially the reserved roads. Directions for the organization of the traffic and the order in which the various troop or wagon trains should reach the passages arranged in the destroyed zone.

k) Supply centers for the large units and the civil population to be organized immediately in the zone reoccupied. Routes for the supply trains.

l) Large units and artillery units kept stationary.

m) Large units and artillery units regrouped to the rear.

III. — ARMY CORPS AND DIVISION PLAN OF ENGAGEMENT.

11? The army corps and divisions assigned to the offensive action draw up their final plans of engagement as soon as their commands and staffs have the reconnaissance and studies of the hostile organizations.

They assemble all the information required by the commands and staffs of the :

Army that drew up the plan of action.

Army corps and divisions that are to hold and organize the front until the attacking troops are brought up.

The plans of engagement should be simple and concise, and should contain only those directions required by the units to whom they are addressed (**), and should not repeat regulation orders.

(*) The large cavalry units (cavalry, corps and cavalry division) should, on receipt of their mission, draw up their own *procedure in case* the enemy withdraws.

(**) See paragraph 106 which is equally applicable to the plan of engagement.

In order to decrease their size and facilitate their study it is suggested that they be in the form of outlines, sketches, and diagrams. The division plan of engagement should always include a diagram, scale 1/10000, giving the distribution of the troops on the day and hour of the attack (D and H).

Plan of engagement.

ARMY CORPS	DIVISION.

120. I. PURPOSE OF THE OFFENSIVE ACTION.

a) Mission of the army corps.	*a)* Mission of the division.
b) Zone of engagement of the army corps.	*b)* Sector of engagement of the division.
c) Mission of adjacent army corps.	*c)* Mission of adjacent divisions.

GENERAL CONDITIONS OF THE EXECUTION.

a) Idea of maneuver.
b) Fixing the time for the preparation and execution of the attacks.
c) Surprise.

121. II. DEFINING THE OBJECTIVES.

a) Objective of the offensive action.
b) Dividing the offensive action into several attacks; directions for the rapid succession of the attacks.

c) Fixing the objectives of the first attack :
Normal objective.
Intermediate objectives.
Possible objectives.
d) Directions for the reconnaissance of the objectives of later attacks.

e) **General plan of the later attacks and for following up the success.**

122. III. GENERAL PLAN FOR THE USE OF THE ATTACK·ING TROOPS.

a) Density of the attacking formations at various parts of the front and their distribution in depth.

Divisions of the first and second lines.

Assaulting troops and reserve troops.

b) Defining the sectors of engagement for the divisions.

b) Defining the sub-sectors of engagement for the regiments and the position of the battalions.

Successive objectives for each division.

Successive objectives for each regiment or battalion.

Maneuver of passing of lines.

Passing of lines.

Schedule for the speed of the advance and schedule alterations.

Varying the speed at different stages of the advance.

Drawing up the schedule and mechanism for its alteration.

General directions for the movements beyond the normal objective.

Detailed arrangements for patrols, reconnaissances, intelligence research detachments, and raiding parties beyond the normal objective; then the advance of the attacking troops or reserves to the possible objective.

Mission of the tactical units charged with covering the flanks of the army corps and the liaison with the adjacent army corps.

Mission of the tactical units charged with covering the flanks of the divisions and the liaison with the adjacent divisions.

c) Distribution and mission of the forces and means at the disposal of the army corps.

c) Distribution and mission of the forces and means at the disposal of the division.

Forces :

Infantry, artillery, aeronautic service, engineers, cavalry, tanks, flame projecting or Z companies, territorial troops, native troops, divisional machine gun companies, liaison detachments.

Means :

Normal and narrow-gauge railways, automobile and wagon trains, ammunition and explosives, engineer materiel, camouflage, material and tools for the repair of communications, equipment of the medical and administrative services.

d) Distribution and mission of the reserves.
Mission of the cavalry.

e) **Plan for bringing the forces and means into action.**

Special directions for the infantry during the preparation (reconnaissances, instruction, training).

Plan for bringing up the infantry.

f) Initial and successive emplacements of the command posts.

g) General precautions against gas.

h) General precautions against aerial bombardment.

123. IV. Plan for using the artillery.

a) Organization of the command. (See supplement I.).— Groups, sub-groups.

Adapting the artillery formation to that of the infantry.
Assigning the missions and objectives.

Normal and possible zones of action.

Cooperation of the groups with one another and with the artillery of adjacent units or of the superior echelon.

Observation (list of terrestrial observation posts and their missions, distribution of the means of aerial observation, map of the ground under observation and not under observation from terrestrial or balloon observation, outline of the observation). (See supplement I).

Liaison (map of the liaison with the observation posts, balloons, wireless posts, command posts, and batteries) (*).

(*) It is indispensable to connect the divisional artillery directly with the nearby terrestrial observation sections of intelligence research and with the sound ranging sections. These liaisons will facilitate the ranging and adjustment of the artillery.

b) Assignment of emplacements :

For the army corps artillery on the engagement terrain of the army corps.

For the divisional artillery on the engagement terrain of the division.

For the army corps artillery on the engagement terrain of adjacent army corps.

For the divisional artillery on the engagement terrain of adjacent divisions.

Reserve emplacements for the artillery of adjacent army corps and the army on the terrain of the army corps.

Reserve emplacements for the artillery of adjacent divisions, the army corps and the army on the terrain of the division.

Bringing up the materiel and groups.

c) Directions for the first trial fires.

d) Directions for the installation and functioning of the meteorological service.

e) Plans for the period of destruction.

Plan for the destruction and neutralization of the artillery : batteries, anti-aircraft batteries, observation posts, balloons, avions.

Distribution of the missions among the army heavy artillery, the army corps heavy artillery and the divisional artillery. (See supplement I.)

Mission of the divisional artillery.

Plan for the destruction of the defensive organizations.

General directions.

Oblique and enfilade action of the divisional artillery for the benefit of the adjacent divisions. Mission of the howitzers and high power heavy artillery mortars.

Maps and diagrams, of the destructions by the :

Trench artillery.
Light artillery.
Heavy howitzers.
(See supplement I.)

Plan for harassing and prohibitive fire.

Communications and constructions.
Transient objectives. (See supplement I.)

Plan of counter-preparation. (See supplement I.)

Prohibitive destructions. — Barrage. — List of concentrations (positions of departure and position of destination).

Plan of false attacks by fire.

f) **Plan for accompanying and protecting the first attack.**

General directions.

Long range action of the army and army corps artillery.

Maps and diagrams for the :

Trench artillery.
Light artillery.
Heavy howitzers.
(See supplement I.)

g) **Plan for the successive artillery positions. (See supplement I.)**

Army and army corps batteries.

Trench artillery.
Light artillery.
Heavy howitzers.

Procedure for shifting the emplacements : relation between the plan for the successive positions and the plan of communications.

Measures for insuring the continuity of artillery fire during the change in emplacements.

h) General directions for the later attacks.

i) Supplying.

Necessary ammunition for the different missions before, during and after the attack.

Special shells.
Sites and organization of depots.
Means for transporting ammunition.

124. IV *bis*. PLAN FOR USING LONG RANGE MACHINE GUNS.

General directions.

Putting the machine guns of the second line division at the disposal of the first line division (later).

a) Composition of the groups.

b) Harassing and prohibitive fire. Fire for preventing the repair of the destructions.

c) Stationary barrages and concentrations.

d) Supplying.

125.   V. PLAN FOR USING THE TANKS.

a) Distribution and use of the tanks assigned to the destruction of defensive organizations.

b) Distribution and use of the tanks assigned to accompany the infantry.

126.   VI. PLAN FOR USING THE ENGINEERS.

Distribution and missions of the army corps and army engineer units.

Distribution and mission of the engineer troops.

127.   VII. PLAN FOR USING THE AERONAUTIC SERVICE.

a) Distribution of the aeronautic materiel.
Emplacement of squadrons and balloons.

b) Directions for the first signs of activity.

c) Use before the attack.
Reconnaissances and photographs. — Directing the destructions.
Ranging with the artillery.

d) Use during the attack.
Infantry liaison.
Reconnaissance and photographs.
Fire control.
Advance of the balloons.

e) General directions for later attacks.

Plan for successive emplacements of the aeronautic service.

128. VIII. PLAN OF LIAISON.

a) Telephone systems completed, under construction, or under consideration, systems for the command, artillery, aeronautic service and the anti-aircraft defense.

b) Assignment of the individual technical characteristics (wave length, pitch, etc.) to the *radio telegraphy posts* (wireless, earth induction) and the time allowed to each post for sending.

c) Organization of the *visual* and *sound signaling* liaison.

d) The code for liaison by *fireworks.*

e) Allotment of *carrier-pigeons.*

f) Characteristic signs of *avions* and *balloons* on missions of liaison; operation of these avions and balloons.

g) Assignment of *call letters* (indicatives).

h) Liaison personnel and *chains* of *couriers.*

i) Exact directions for the *lines of communications, intelligence centers, telephone* and *visual signaling centrals.*

j) Detaching the units of workmen.

k) Materiel supply.

129. IX. PLAN OF INTELLIGENCE RESEARCH.

a) Special arrangements for hastening the transmission and use of information.

Have direct communication between the various organs (*).

Infantry intelligence service :

Division and army corps intelligence service (Staff).

Division topographical service and army corps topographical service.

Artillery intelligence service, and aeronautic intelligence service.

(*) These direct communications should never do away with the regular communications prescribed by « The instruction on intelligence research ».

Army topographical sections.

b) Detaching of certain organs of the army artillery intelligence service to the army corps artillery intelligence service. (Terrestrial observation sections of intelligence research and sound ranging sections.)

General directions for the artillery intelligence service and the aviation intelligence service.

c) Duties of the intelligence sections (Staff).

Instructions to the various intelligence research organs :

Instructions to the army corps topographical sections.

Daily conferences between the research organs.

Instructions to the division topographical sections.

Centralization and use of information.

Drawing up the publications indicated in the *Instruction* on battle maps, maps, and special diagrams, and at times other charts, maps and sketches.

130. X. PLAN OF COMMUNICATIONS, SUPPLY AND EVACUATIONS.

A) **Communications.**

a) Use of railroads (normal, metric, 60 centimeter, 40 centimeter).

b) Use of roads (reserved roads, one way traffic).

c) Automobile routes.

d) Policing the roads, bridges, paths and the rear of the battlefield. Cleaning up the rear of the battlefield.

e) Duties of the provost with respect to communications and military police.

B) **Supply.**

a) Assigning the stations.

b) Artillery services.

Warehouses . . . . . . } site and organization,
Ammunition depots. . . } amount of supplies.

Assigning motor-trucks and wagons for transport.

c) Engineer service.

Warehouses . . . . . . } site and organization,
Depots . . . . } amount of supplies.

Assigning motor trucks and wagons for transport.

d) Administrative service :

Food . . . . } site and organization,
Water . . . . } amount of supplies.

Assigning auto-trucks and wagons for transport.

e) Medical service :

Materiel depots. . . . . } site and emplacement,
} amount of supplies.

C) **Evacuations.**

a) Assignment of ambulances, hospitals and evacuation hospitals.

b) Detailed directions for the evacuations.

D) **Prisoners.**

Movements and formation of trains of prisoners.

E) **Directions for the advance.**

a) Narrow-gauge railways and roads to be improved.

b) Assigning working units and the use of auto-trucks and wagons for transport.

c) Materiel supply for advancing the warehouses and depots.

131. XI. Plan of the works.

a) Arrangements for terminating or completing the *forward works.*

Offensive organizations.

Organs of command.
Artillery emplacements.
Landing stations, hangars and auxiliary ground.
Depots.
Camps and shelters.
Liaison.
Communications.
Water supply.
Medical service.
Prison camps.

b) Later, the completion of the *rear works*.

c) Program of the *works after the attack :*

Organization of the captured position.
Successive artillery positions.
Advancing the liaison, communications and supplies.

d) Assigning the work places to the :

Troops in the sector when the plan is drawn up.
Attacking troops . . . . ⎰ (before, during and after the
Special units of workmen. ⎱   attack).

132. XII. PROCEDURE IN CASE OF AN ENEMY'S
WITHDRAWAL.

a) Recognizing an intended withdrawal.

b) Mission of the troops assigned to the later advance :

Defining the zones of advance of the division.	Defining the zones of advance of the regiments.

c) Lines of communications.

d) Directions for the first advance :

Debouching and advancing.
Mission of the artillery moving with the infantry.
Mission of the artillery that retain their initial emplacements.
Mission of the assaulting artillery.

e) Transversals at which the liaisons of the advancing units are insured.

f) Mission of the aeronautic service :

Reconnaissance of the enemy and his halting positions.
Reconnaissance of the first friendly lines.
Transmission of information and orders.

g) Mission of the engineers.

h) Mission of the cavalry.

i) Assigning units of workmen :

For the extension and improvement of communications and roads.

For advancing the materiel, ammunition and supplies
For shifting the artillery.
For extending narrow-gauge railways.

j) Extending the traffic facilities, especially the reserved roads. Directions of the organization of the traffic.

k) Supply centers for the large units and the civil population to be organized immediately in the zone occupied : double traffic roads for the supply trains.

l) Units kept stationary.

m) Units to be re-grouped to the rear.

CHAPTER VI.

WORKS. — RECONNAISSANCES. — DESTRUCTIONS.

I. — WORKS.

133. The terrain chosen for an offensive action should be organized to facilitate not only the first attack but also the rapid, continuous and orderly development of the general action. It should permit :

1) The construction of a system of communications pushed as close to the first lines as possible and capable of being extended into the captured ground.

2) The rapid installation of the artillery.

3) The rapid installation of the aeronautic service.

4) Bringing up the infantry, under cover, facing the objectives and at a proper distance from the enemy; the rapid and orderly debouching.

5) Unfailing liaison.

6) Convenient supply system.

7) Rapid evacuations.

Communications.

134. The system of communication consists of :

a) Normal and metric railways.

b) Narrow-gauge railways (60 and 40 centimeters).

c) Roads (reserved roads, one way roads, automobile circuits).

d) Dirt roads and tracks.

Building these communications is almost entirely a part of the rear works. They should therefore be built far in advance by the offensive resources of the fronts concerned.

New works will be necessary immediately before the attack, but these will be assigned to special units.

It will be necessary to extend all the communications as near as possible to the parallels of departure and to provide in detail for their development beyond these parallels by :

Terrestrial and aerial reconnaissances and studies of contour maps, battle maps and photographs so as to determine the trace of these extensions.

Materiel and camouflage depots in the zone of the departure parallels for the purpose of facilitating the crossing of trenches, approach trenches and streams by the artillery, tanks and vehicles.

The collecting and camouflage of various supplies of materiel in order to insure without delay the entension of trails and narrow-gauge tracks and roads and railroads.

Training numerous units of workmen for their special work (methodical organization of the work places, assignment and mission of the officers, non-commissioned officers and crews, etc.).

Position of these workmen at the beginning of the attack.

The command will pay special attention to the extension of the communications and to the special intensive training of the work units.

Installation of artillery.

135. The plan for the offensive preparation of the front considers the later reinforcement by providing for :

The emplacements of batteries, command and observation posts, and the liaison between batteries, command and observation posts.

The ammunition depots and the trace of the communications connecting them with the batteries (roads, trails, narrow-gauge railways).

The sites of the ammunition sections.

Similar works will be executed by the troops in the sector.

The army topographical sections choose the reference marks on the terrain for the orientation of batteries.

In each sector of the attack it is necessary to complete this preparation and to adapt it to the artillery assigned to the attack.

With this in view it is advantageous to detach officers to the artillery staffs in the sector. These officers will take care of this detailed preparation.

They will pay special attention to the :

a) Assembling and distribution of the camouflage and construction materiel.

b) Materiel for gas protection and the necessary spare parts.

c) Topographical determination of battery emplacements and observation posts; staking out the ranging directions.

d) Connecting the emplacements of heavy batteries with the 60 centimeter tracks (*).

(*) Sections of 60 or 40 centimeter track or sidings near the positions; assembling the various mat riel, straight and curved sections.

e) Choice and distribution of the emplacements for the echelons; choose solid ground, especially for the sites of the automobile units; improvement of the approaches.

f) Cooperation with the telegraph service for the construction of the telephone lines; adapting it to the distribution of the artillery (*).

g) Organization of parks; their supply and repair parts of the different materiel (**).

h) Supplementary supplies of ammunition (***).

i) Choosing elements from the artillery of the sector to guide the units into the sector on their arrival.

On coming into the sector the artillery command considers the advanced positions to be occupied by the light and heavy batteries before or during the attack and the emplacements to be reserved for the assaulting artillery.

The working places and the various constructions are camouflaged by special workmen, by the units themselves, or by the units themselves with the help of auxiliary workmen.

Installation of the aeronautic service.

136. A) Aviation.

1) The *organization of the aviation grounds* should be made long in advance (****).

The specified grounds will be :

Extensive so as to facilitate landing and avoid congestion even with an increase in the number of units.

(*) Calculate the number of circuits liberally. Experience shows that the estimates are always beneath the requirements.

(**) Assignment of detache dofficers to look into the situation of the troops on the spot.

(***) These supplies will constitute a reserve and will make it possible to supply the units with the ammunition appropriate to the various kinds of fire.

(****) Nevertheless in view of the importence of the works it will be difficult to realize them completely beforehand by the offensive équipment.

Cleared and perfectly level so as to decrease the number of accidents.

Served by good approaches :

Toward the rear for supplies.
Toward the front for liaison.

2) *Erection of hangars and cantonments.*

If these can not be put up several months in advance, they should be built only several days before the arrival of the squadrons.

a) Have the squadrons separated from one another so as to maintain their unity and decrease the effect of bombardment.

b) In each squadron keep the hangars and cantonments separated so as to minimize the effect of fire.

All constructions will be carefully camouflaged.

3) The *telephone liaison* indicated by the *"Instruction on Liaison"* should be organized as soon as possible.

4) The *advanced grounds* will be organized :

a) To permit communication with the command posts on landing.

b) To permit the aviation grounds being moved forward

137. B) Aerostation.

The works necessary for the aerostation service includes :
The organization of camps and ascending stations.
The organization of roads between the camps and ascending stations and the forward roads.
The supply of the materiel necessary for crossing the lines.
The construction of the first position telephone centrals and advanced centrals.
The construction of the telephone system.

Installation and debouching of the infantry.

138. The operations for the installation and debouching of the infantry for the first attacks include :

Parallels of departure and shelters.
Assembling places.
Approach and communication trenches.

A) PARALLELS OF DEPARTURE AND SHELTERS.

The parallels of departure should be traced and organized to permit the assaulting troops to debouch *facing their objective* under the best conditions of rapidity and cohesion.

As a rule the distance from our most advanced parallel to the enemy's first line should not exceed 400 or 500 meters so as to protect the assaulting troops from the hostile artillery barrages. It should not be less than 200 meters so as to permit our own barrage preparation and counter-preparation fire (*).

These two limits may require that :

a) The front be altered to place the troops opposite to their objective.

b) One or several parallels be dug in front of the first line at parts of the front where adverse trenches are too far apart.

To retain the benefit of surprise, these works will not be built unless the offensive preparation of the front permits their construction long in advance. A less completely organized base of departure will be compensated for by the density and depth of the barrages accompanying and protecting the debouch of the infantry.
· Whenever possible have each wave issue from open ground and not from the parallel where it was formed. Each parallel is thus equipped with sortie steps and bridging ladders for the rear waves.

(*) In reality the distance between the hostile front lines is often less than 200 meters. Certain parallels and approach trenches are then evacuated during the period of preparation.

The successive waves may all debouch from the advanced parallel (*). The number of approach trenches leading to this parallel should then be increased.

A combination of these two methods may be used.

Take into consideration the. breaches made in the entanglement and adapt the arrangement ·of the parallels of departure to the plan for opening breaches.

The construction of numerous *dugouts* in the zone of the departure parallels facilitates assembling the troops towards the front and consequently their debouch.

139. B) ASSEMBLING PLACES.

Assembling places are used to bring together the support troops and reserves under cover.

They may be in trenches or under natural cover or may be built of any emergency material.

They should however :

Be built long in advance so as not to betray the offensive project at the last moment.

Be arranged so as not to entail an excessive breaking up of the units.

Offer easy egress toward the open field and toward the approaches.

Include *dugouts*.

The site of the assembling places depends on the mission of the troops who are to use them. The slowness with which one moves under cover in approach trenches and the advantage of having a minimum passage over fire swept ground demand that these assembling places be near the parallels of departure.

140. C) APPROACH TRENCHES.

The approach trenches should form a network in which

_____

(*) This method is to be used when the zone.of the parallels of departure contains obstacles that can not l e eliminated.

the main lines used for reference can easily be distinguished on the map and identified on the terrain.

The system comprises :

Main approach trenches, whose development toward the rear depends on :

The depth and formation of the troops.
The intended shifting of troops during the engagement.
The topography of the terrain.
The personnel and time available for their construction.

Secondary approach trenches whose number depends on the attacking formation and increases towards the front from the assembling places to the advanced parallel.

As a rule the main approach trenches are subdivided into *evacuation* trenches and approaches *leading forward.* These should permit easy passage for the stretcher bearers.

Approach trenches should be named to avoid confusion.
Names on battle maps should not be changed.
Main approach trenches should be named or numbered different from secondary approach trenches.

Approach trenches should have a regular trace so as to minimize the length of passage and the chances of error.
They should have dugouts for the detached men and, at regular intervals, side passages, sortie steps and ramps for the evacuation trenches.
They are doubled by tracks and together with the parallels are liberally sign-posted.
Sign-posts are necessary at the entries to approach trenches, at crossings, at sortie steps and ramps. The shapes, dimensions and colors are different for the parallels, primary and secondary approach trenches.
Placards and arrows indicate the direction of important points such as command posts, observation posts, first aid stations, and depots.
Traffic is subject to a strict discipline and controlled by orders.
Constituted detachments are charged with the mainte-

nance and repair of the approach trenches. They also enforce the traffic regulations.

Units of workmen are assigned to extend the main approach trenches as the attack advances.

Command posts, observation posts, and liaison.

141. *a*) The construction of command and observation posts is very important. Command posts should be built near the observation posts and should have good communication with the main approach trenches.

They are marked by conspicuous signs. They are arranged so as to be easily found even by liaison agents who are strangers in that sector.

The successive command posts for the same echelon of the command are planned and constructed in advance.

b) Buried telephone lines should be built immediately so as to have liaison with the command posts of the first line.

There are special units of workmen for advancing the materiel extending the liaison as the attack advances.

Supplies.

142. Build depots for food, water, ammunition, explosives, tools, materiel, gas apparatus, etc... as far forward as the zone of the parallels of departure.

All depots should be of the same type of construction and should be built by skilled crews. The sites should be marked by signs and should be familiar to all the units affected.

A special personnel is assigned to guard them.

Units are designated for the transport of materiel and supplies as soon as the advance begins.

Evacuations.

143. First aid stations are placed so as to permit the arrival and evacuation of wounded without hindering the circulation.

Passages for ambulances should be pushed forward as far as possible.

The plan of evacuation is followed with respect to the previsions for insuring good medical service from the first lines to the evacuation hospitals.

II. — RECONNAISSANCES.

144. The command, staffs and troops occupying the fronts chosen for an offensive action or designated for the attack should make it their duty to become informed of the enemy and the terrain on which the action will take place.

Intelligence research.

145. A) SUBJECT MATTER.

a) The **infantry** and the defensive elements of the hostile front :

Defensive organizations :

    Auxiliary defenses.
    Flanking organs.
    Trenches, approaches, works, organized mine craters and shell holes, concrete shelters and dugouts, mines.
    Machine gun, infantry artillery, and trench mortar emplacements.
    Depots of materiel, ammunition and explosives.

Command, observation and look-out posts.
Telephone and visual signaling centrals.
Life of the infantry, the method of holding the ground, the routes of reliefs and supply parties.
Kitchens, camps and billets.
Distribution centers for food and materiel.

b) The **artillery** :

Emplacements of the batteries; their occupations (number of guns, calibres, anti-aircraft guns and anti-tank guns).

Ammunition depots.

Artillery command and observation posts.

Life of the artillery, its methods, customary objectives, zones of barrage and harassing fire, codes and call letters, movements, supply routes.

c) The **aeronautic service :**

Landing grounds for avions.

Points of ascension and camps for balloons.

Life of the aviation, methods of combat, bombardement, reconnaissance and artillery control, hours of flight, materiel, all phases of the local tactics.

d) The **communications :**

Trails, dirt roads, roads and traffic by way of roads.

Normal and narrow-gauge roads and their traffic.

e) The **rear :**

Successive organized positions.

Military and industrial organizations.

Movements of the civil population.

f) **Signs of attack or of an enemy's retreat :**

Reinforcements and movements.

Fires, destructions, and other signs.

g) The **terrain** (topographical characteristics, nature of the earth, facilities for movement at various times) :

The ground as seen from the position of departure.

The ground between the position of departure and the normal objective (terrestrial observation, relief maps, aerial observation and photographs).

The ground beyond the normal objective (theoretical study of hostile counter-attacks).

146. B) Procedure.

The observation and intelligence research work is indicated for each echelon by the *plan for intelligence research and use.* Measures are taken to facilitate the rapid diffusion of information to the interested units.

Observation should be *continuous* : The units in the sector at the beginning of the work draw up complete reports for the benefit of the units who will be called to enter this sector by the attack.

The *command and the staffs of the attacking troops* come into the sector as soon as possible after the units and inform themselves of the conditions, take over the orders, receive the reports and intelligence data, and supervise the preparation of the observation organs and the intelligence research.

They familiarize themselves with the main objects of this service.

They inspect the observation posts of the command, the principal infantry observation posts, the principal artillery intelligence or control posts, and are careful not to attract the enemy's attention.

They see to it that the service is well supervised, that the *plan of intelligence research* is rigidly followed and that the improvements deemed necessary are immediately carried out.

They order aerial reconnaissances so as to take into consideration the panoramic appearance of the terrain and the details of certain organizations. These also permit observation of the ground hidden from terrestrial posts.

The staff officers, intelligence officers (staff), topographical officers, certain officers of the artillery and aviation, intelligence service, artillery intelligence service, and the aeronautic intelligence service precede their units and, together with the officers of the troops in the sector, work up the photographs and the summary diagrams by the aerial photography sections and army corps topographical sections, the final form of the battle maps and the contour maps.

Each service completes the intelligence reports received from the units in the sector and verifies the choice and organization of the observation posts.

The chiefs of staff of the attacking units follow this preparatory work and the organization of liaison and lend all the assistance possible to the intelligence officers of the various arms.

The army commander sees to it that the units in the sector hand over to the attacking units all of the orders and materiel pertaining to the sector.

Engagement reconnaissances.

147. In addition to the regular intelligence research, the officers and non-commissioned officers of all attacking units make the reconnaissances preparatory to their engagement.

These reconnaissances are of two kinds :

148. A) RECONNAISSANCES PREPARATORY TO THE FORMULATING OF THE PLAN OF ENGAGEMENT. — The command, the staffs (*), the officers and non-commissioned officers of all attacking troops should first of all become familiar with the terrain with respect to :

The friendly terrain, where the offensive organizations are built and where the attacking troops will be assembled.

The hostile ground containing the objectives.

The choice of the points of direction and the determination of the angles of march.

149. B) DETAILED RECONNAISSANCES PRECEDING THE ENGAGEMENT. — These reconnaissances are made during the entire preparation :

Whether the troops are still in the rear (and in this case the staff, officers and non-commissioned officers are usually brought up to their position where they remain).

Or the final attacking formation has been assumed.

(*) The command and the staffs who precede the troops in the zone of attack, should *act immediately* even before they can occupy the sites and command posts that will later be assigned to them.

They should be able when the troops arrive, to put them in place in the shortest time possible and to start them off on their mission.

It is recommended that the staff be provisionally installed in automobiles with a telephone line to the nearest central.

They are completed by a study of vertical and oblique photographs, relief maps, photographs of relief maps, panoramic diagrams and battle maps. These maps and diagrams are furnished by the intelligence officers who precede the units, by the army corps topographical service and the division topographical service.

150. C) ATTACK DIAGRAMS AND EXERCISES. — The attack diagrams are made in the camps or near the rest cantonments where the attacking units are stationed.

They show the points and lines of direction, the lines indicating the intermediate objectives, the normal objective, the possible objective and the passing of lines.

The exercises familiarize the troops with all the details of the operation, including the cleaning of the trenches.

The diagrams, notes on photographs and large scale maps are drawn up for the same purpose beginning with the subaltern officers and non-commissioned officers.

Photographic slides may be very useful.

Controlling the destructions.

151. The last phase of the engagement reconnaissances deals mostly with the control of the destructions, by the infantry intelligence service, the artillery intelligence service and the aeronautic intelligence service. The infantry intelligence service deals mostly with the destruction of the auxiliary defenses and the hostile bombing posts nearest the parallels of departure (*).

The command, the staff and all of the officers and non-commissioned officers also participate in this control. The control is completed by patrols which advance during the night or fog to the close objectives of the destruction fire.

(*) During the period of destruction the enemy will attempt to advance machine guns or bombing posts which escape destruction and are to break up the attack as soon as it is launched. The infantry intelligence service assigns the destruction of these machine guns or bombing posts to the trench artillery, machine guns, or bombers.

The command of all echelons should seek, transmit and use all the information arising from this control.

At the end of each day, there will be drawn up, according to the *"Instruction on battle maps, maps and special diagrams"*, diagrams to the scale of 1/1000 showing the progress of the destructions.

Mission of the aeronautic service.

152. In each large unit the aeronautic service is an essential organ for intelligence research and reconnaissances.

Its proper efficiency demands that the personnel of the observation and balloon squadrons be perfectly familiar with the terrain. These aeronautic units should be brought up before the large units to which they are assigned.

Their officers, non-commissioned officers and observers should frequently visit and keep in constant liaison with the staff and the troops. During these visits they prepare the execution of the liaison and firing missions and diffuse the air intelligence.

The photographic sections should be ready to comply with all demands made on them. The observers should assist the staff and the officers in the examination of photographs by adding remarks and notes arising from their direct observation of the terrain.

III. — DESTRUCTIONS.

Destruction by artillery fire.

153. A) Destruction fire, harassing fire, and neutralization fire against hostile observation posts, avions, and balloons.

a) **Destruction fire.** — *Destruction fire* will be executed

on an *isolated battery* only when sure of the objective (*);
*when the fire is accurately adjusted, controlled throughout
its duration, and executed with abundance of ammunition.*

As the value of fire lies in its accuracy, and as the
accuracy depends on continuous observation, it is not
sufficient to adjust the fire once for all. The fire may
vary because of a change in atmospheric pressure, in wind,
because of the heating of the gun, etc. *The observation
and the control should be permanent.*

Destruction fire against a single battery should be
continued until the desired result has been obtained.
Several rounds is not sufficient for effective results, but a
large number of rounds accurately fired and calculated
according to the calibre will achieve the desired result.

Zone fire is less efficient in its consumption of ammunition. Notwithstanding this objection, it should be used
often for various reasons (uncertainty as to the emplacement of the objective, lack of observation organs, reducing
the delays in the preparation, etc.). The effect of this fire
is considerable when concentrated on known *nests of
batteries.*

Destruction fire should also be executed on *anti-aircraft
and anti-tank guns.*

154. *b)* **Harassing fire. — Preventing the repair of
destructions. —** A continuous harassing fire, night and
day, should follow the destruction fire so as to prevent
the enemy from repairing the damage, supplying his troops,
and changing positions.

This harassing fire is valuable because of the damage to
materiel and the physical and moral strain on the personnel.

155. *c)* **Neutralization fire.**

Neutralization fire is used to momentarily silence hostile

(*) The destruction of an isolated battery should be undertaken only when
the emplacement is clearly defined and when it is certain that the battery
is occupied (flashes, smoke, powder).

batteries that are not destroyed. Special shells (*), high explosive shells and shrapnel are used.

Neutralization fire on batteries or nests of batteries should be intense so as to prevent the enemy from using the pieces and to cut his communications. The fire is controlled as much as possible.

156. *d)* **Fire on observation posts.** — Artillery fire will be used to destroy or neutralize terrestrial observation posts. With the help of the combat avions, artillery fire will be used to destroy balloons and avions (**) or to hold them at a distance.

Fire against terrestrial observation posts should be especially violent toward the end of the preparation. It includes the use of special shells, when the weather and the terrain are favorable, high explosive shells against dugout entrances and against communications, time shells and smoke shells for hindering observation.

157. *e)* **Organization and control of the combat.**

The combat against the enemy's artillery is organized and led :

In the army, by the army artillery commander who controls the use of the army artillery, assigns a zone of action to each army corps and coordinates the action of the army corps according to the instructions of the army commander.

In the army corps, by the army corps artillery commander who assigns the zones of action of the heavy artillery groups and later of the divisional artillery, and

---

(*) The special shells are especially effective and their use for neutralization fire gives excellent results when the weather is favorable.

A sufficiently prolonged action may bring about the deterioration of the gas masks by using up the spare gas mask cartridges and thus lead to the destruction of the personnel.

(**) The combat against avions devolves mainly on the artillery and machine guns of the anti-aircraft defense. Avions flying low over the first lines should be fired at by all the army corps artillery in range and by the infantry and artillery machine guns.

who coordinates the action of these groups according to the instructions of the army corps commander.

The army and army corps commanders and the army and army corps artillery commanders should continually control (*) the action of the counter-battery artillery.

158. *Army.*

The army commander assigns a normal zone of action and a possible zone of action (**).

The army artillery commander together with the army corps artillery commanders provides that the hostile batteries situated in the normal zone of an army corps and firing on adjacent army corps be subjected to neutralization fire.

The army heavy artillery batteries are distributed in groups. These groups are assigned to the army corps and are immediately under the army corps artillery commanders.

The army artillery commander intervenes only when the groups become unavailable for duty. In this case he supplies the army corps with other batteries from the army.

The heavy counter-battery artillery of an army corps may be supported by that of adjacent army corps. This reinforcement is provided for in advance. The necessary liaison is established so that the adjacent army corps can reinforce one another on demand..

159. *Army corps.*

The counter battery artillery of each army corps works for the benefit of its corps and of other army corps.

The army corps artillery commander prepares a general

(*) After each series of destruction fire, photographs are taken and rapidly transmitted to the artillery commanders of the army and army corps. These photographs show the effects of the fire and enable the daily plan of destruction to be drawn up.

(**) The possible zones of action are made to include all the hostile batteries that are known to fire habitually in the zone of the army corps interested. It is always more certain and more rapid to have each army corps take care of the opposing batteries that hinder it than to ask their destruction or neutralization by adjacent army corps.

counter-battery program according to the instructions of the army corps commander.

He has under his orders to carry out this program the army corps batteries not assigned to divisions, the army artillery batteries detached to the army corps, the howitzer batteries that the army corps commander decides to select temporarily from the divisional artillery of destruction (*) and finally all the army corps artillery.

The army corps artillery commander insures intimate liaison and cooperation between the heavy artillery and the divisional artillery. He sees to it that the plans for destruction never deprive the divisional infantry and artillery of the counter-battery support, when exposed to hostile fire.

The *program of destruction* should take into consideration the possibilities of enfilade or oblique fire on batteries or groups of batteries close to one another, and consequently more important results with less ammunition.

It indicates the batteries, lines or nests of batteries to be destroyed by each group, the order of urgency of these destructions, the harassing fire during the day and night, and the batteries that are to be kept available for action against the hostile batteries that may later be discovered.

This program provides for destruction fire against observation posts.

The order of urgency of the destruction fire is not *invariable*. It depends on the activity of the hostile batteries. Destruction fire should be directed first on those batteries firing the same day and others known to be occupied.

The *program of neutralization* indicates the batteries to be neutralized by each group of the normal zone and the possible zones of action.

160. The programs of destruction and neutralization

(*) The divisional artillery assists in the counter-battery fire, especially in the period preceding the destruction of the defensive organizations. The army corps artillery commander controls its use so that these guns can immediately resume their essential missions of barrage and counter-preparation fire.

are kept to date by means of information received by the intelligence sections of the staffs and the artillery intelligence service.

When approved by the army corps commander, the destruction and the neutralization programs are given over for execution to the commanders of the army heavy artillery groups, of the army corps heavy artillery (use of this heavy artillery) and the division commanders (use of howitzer batteries and perhaps the light artillery).

The commanders of the army heavy artillery groups, of the army corps heavy artillery, and of the divisional artillery, draw up each day their programs for the next day, using the above indicated destruction and neutralization programs as outlines. These programs deal with the destruction fire to be executed, the batteries that are to participate, and the terrestrial and aerial observation posts at their disposal.

They indicate the batteries or battalions that are to remain prepared for special missions or for neutralization fire against batteries discovered at the last moment.

161. Notwithstanding the various firing programs, the artillery should immediately fire on all batteries that are signalled as being in action. The assignment of a normal zone of action to each group takes care of th's.

162. B) Destruction of the defensive organizations.

The *destruction of defensive organizations* is taken care of by the divisional artillery whose composition varies with the various missions.

Because of the numerous missions of the heavy howitzers, it will be necessary to use trench artillery as much as possible, especially at the beginning of an engagement or of every important phase of the engagement.

The effectiveness of the fire depends on the accuracy of the adjustments and on their permanent control.

The destruction fire should be accompanied by a raking fire around the objective so as to reach the personnel who take refuge in shell holes.

All destruction fire should be followed by *fire to prevent the repair of the damage.*

The artillery officers in charge of the destruction of the hostile organizations keep in constant liaison with the officers of the infantry facing these organizations. The latter inform them of all the details and follow the destructions which are verified by the intelligence officers and patrols.

163. The *division commander* controls the program and the rate of the destruction fire. This fire should begin with those objectives whose repair is most difficult and whose destruction most vital (*).

The division commander indicates the fire for the prevention of repair of these objectives (**).

When necessary he modifies the first line positions of the infantry or has certain parts of these lines momentarily evacuated so that the destruction of the hostile works near our own lines may proceed without accidents to us.

164. The *divisional artillery commander* draws up a detailed plan for using the materiel, which is approved by the division commander. He assigns the objectives to each group or unit of light, trench or heavy artillery, allots the ammunition and the terrestrial and aerial observation posts (***). He arranges for the prohibitive fire on the destructions.

The destructions should be directed and verified by the command. With this in mind the division commander has photographs made of the results of the destruction fire. He examines these together with the commander of the divisional artillery (****).

(*) Economize in ammunition by not beginning the execution of the breaches too soon as they are easily repaired.

(**) For this prohibitive fire it is advantageous to use machine guns and 75's together with several volleys of heavy artillery even if the objective has been destroyed.

(***) This allotment should be made according to a program sufficiently flexible to permit the full use of all hours favorable for observation.

(****) The best method of verifying destruction fire is by photography. The observations made by aerial and terrestrial observers also help in this

After examining these photographs and the reports of infantry and artillery observers the divisional artillery commander draws up in the evening the order for the next day. This order assigns the work for all the groups and units (*).

He requisitions from the army corps artillery commander the use of the heavy calibre guns and assigns the objectives to them.

The plan for using the destruction artillery should be *kept to date according to the local conditions, the results obtained and the new works constructed.*

165. The *army and army corps commanders* follow the destruction work of the divisions very closely. They insure the good execution of fire by personal visits or by visits of their staff or staff officers of the army and army corps artillery.

166. C) Fire on the enemy's communications and quarters.

This fire includes :

Destruction fire.
Harassing or prohibitive fire.

a) **Destruction fire** should be executed as indicated for destruction fire on defensive organizations. Special attention is paid to quarters, depots, and watering places.

---

verification. All information received by the artillery and infantry observers should be rapidly assembled and sent each evening to the division staff. This intelligence completes and, when atmospheric conditions are unfavorable, replaces the photos.

Photographs should be studied with great care as the conditions of lighting of the terrain have a great influence on the impression derived from photographs. The photographs should be interpreted by skilled men well equipped. Interpretations in badly lighted command posts are often false.

(*) This work should be very carefully organized if it is desired to avoid delays in the daily fire. The avion and balloon observers, for each of the groups whose fire they control are supplied with a list of adjustments and an order of urgency which can be modified by a telephone call. The orders for the fire of the first hour of the day can thus be given sufficiently in advance.

b) **Harassing fire** is used against stationary personnel (in trenches, camps, billets, distribution centers, etc.).

c) **Prohibitive fire** is used to prevent or at least hinder the circulation of the enemy (in approach trenches, on trails, roads or railways).

The firing procedure is constantly varied (*). It should be based on the customary actions of the enemy and therefore necessitates a constant research and a judicious use of intelligence (**).

When properly executed, *harassing and especially prohibitive fire causes great material and moral effects.*

The projectiles used for harassing and prohibitive fire are *time shrapnel* and *high explosive* shells with instantaneous fuses.

Special shells in great numbers and in favorable weather give good results against sheltered districts such as woods and bottoms of ravines. (Lachrymatory shells are recommended because of their persistent action.)

Harassing and prohibitive fire should be well adjusted and frequently verified. These operations necessitate the cooperation of balloons, avions and the terrestrial observation intelligence service (adjustment by bursts in air).

Enfilade fire is especially advantageous.

167. D) Fire on transient objectives.

Arrangements are made to open immediate fire upon transient objectives such as workmen, marching troops, gatherings, convoys, trains, etc...

These objectives are fired upon by rapid fire materiel and guns having a large horizontal field of fire.

A number of batteries of 75's and heavy long guns (105, 140, 155 Filloux, 160) are assigned to take care of

(*) At times a passage that is well marked may be systematically spared so as to attract the hostile traffic to it. The directions of the counter-attacks can thus be localized during an advance. Concentrations prepared in advance on the zones formerly free of fire have several times permitted the enemy's counter-attacks to be broken by a sudden and heavy action.

(**) Questioning of prisoners, study of photographs, etc.

transient objectives in addition to their other missions. A zone of action is assigned to each of these batteries. Each of these batteries is in communication with a permanent wireless receiving set.

These zones of action and the call letters of the corresponding receiving sets are made known to all aerial observers in the sector who can thus call the batteries into action rapidly.

168. E) MISCELLANEOUS KINDS OF FIRE.

During the period of destruction, the artillery may be called upon to execute :

Counter-preparation and barrage fire.

False attack fire to deceive the enemy and lead him to reveal the batteries or machine guns which he always tries to keep concealed until the last moment.

Special shell fire on points where many troops are assembled;

Concentration fire.

It is advantageous to repeat the accompanying fire with avion control the day before or two days before the attack by the artillery of each division and by the batteries of the divisional artillery.

The aeronautic service before and during the period of destruction.

169. 1) *Before the period of destructions.*

As long as the enemy is in doubt as to the zones of attack, the command should avoid revealing the importance of his aeronautic resources.

He maintains a permanent air police with the *minimum of materiel.*

170. As soon as the artillery begins its work, all means should be brought into play to acquire superiority in the air.

Profit by the periods when the hostile aeronautic service is inferior to ours by attacking in force the main part of his combat aviation. Bombard his important points during the day; make repeated and long raids within his lines, organize numerous photographic missions; and attack his balloons and aviation grounds.

These operations are combined with important action by combat patrols organized to obtain superiority over the enemy.

For some of these operations, such as the attack on balloons and aviation grounds, the commander will give the squadrons the support of the light, heavy and high power heavy artillery which will concentrate their fire on these objectives and on the destruction or neutralization of the hostile anti-aircraft batteries.

171. 2) *During the period of destruction.*

In order to obtain the best control service from the aerial observation it is necessary :

a) To draw up a fire program so as to keep the army corps aeronautic commander in touch with the urgency of the missions and thus enable him to use the atmospheric conditions to the best advantage.

b) To engage the enemy's aeronautic service so as to insure the security of the observation avions and balloons.

This security will only be insured by the distinctly offensive action of most of the squadrons and by leaving only the necessary materiel for missions of immediate protection. The raids will nevertheless be shorter and less frequent. The offensive will be carried out by a system of high and low patrols permanently kept over the enemy's territory in a zone indicated by the army commander. These patrols will attack all hostile avions that are met.

172. The aeronautic service draws up a program of destruction for its bombing squadrons.

They assist in the combat against the enemy's artillery by a sustained action against his supply organs (stations, ammunition depots, formations, parks, etc...).

Night attacks with bombs and machine guns on these

objectives will have a very great harassing effect on the hostile artillery and machine guns.

Night bombardments must at the same time give rise to reconnaissances.

Participation of machine guns in harassing and prohibitive fire.

173. The divisional machine gun units should :

Play an active part in prohibiting communications.
Cooperate in harassing the troops and batteries.
Carry on fire for the prevention of repairs.
They can exert a very great material and moral effect.

CHAPTER VII.

BRINGING UP THE INFANTRY.

174. The infantry of the attack should be brought up as late as possible so as to be *fresh and rested at the moment of assault.*

They should also be *trained and instructed for this assault.* They should be familiar with the terrain and in close liaison with all the elements that are to support or accompany their advance.

These two conditions are taken care of by the *plans for bringing up the infantry.*

Bringing up the infantry when the preparation for the attack can be realized long in advance.

175. It has been shown in Chapter II that the best formation for attack is the one in which the army corps can be engaged *in square formation* with :

Two divisions for the first line attack.
Two divisions for the second line attack.

In this case the troops will be brought up in three phases :

176. 1) The *divisions designated for the first line attack* will be brought into the sector several weeks (about six) before the attack. Their transport will be regulated to this effect.

They should be echeloned in depth so as not to increase the density of the position at this time.

They should be left in the sector long enough (about 2 weeks) so that each battalion passes at least 4 or 5 days in the first line.

Allow these divisions to become familiar with the ground, to establish their liaisons, to found their intelligence services, to help in building the works, to make the necessary improvements, to choose their points of direction, to study the photos, relief maps and battle maps on the spot, to draw up their diagrams, etc...

177. 2) The *divisions designated for the second line attack* will relieve the former divisions (about 4 weeks before the attack).

They will have the sector until the week before the attack and will retain a formation such that the density of the front will not be increased.

They will take over all the orders of the first line attacking divisions, especially the intelligence services and the improvements necessary to the works.

They will perform the reconnaissances and studies that the plans of engagement require from second line attacking divisions, especially with respect to the *maneuvers of passing of lines* indicated in these plans.

They will indicate the procedure when the mission of the first line infantry divisions devolves on the second line divisions, as in the case of an enemy's withdrawal during the preparation.

They will follow and control the destruction for their own benefit and for that of the first line attacking divisions.

During this time, the first line attacking divisions will be withdrawn to the rear for rest and for methodical training and instruction.

They will follow up their instruction by attack exercises

in which the role of the officers and non-commissioned officers will be studied with the greatest care.

They will detach to the divisions designated for the second line attack liaison officers with the staff, artillery, intelligence or liaison services, but they should not hinder the rest of the officers and men of these services. At this moment rest is necessary for all echelons. They will insure reconnaissances and later patrols, so as to control the destructions by terrestrial and aerial observation.

178. 3) The *divisions designated for the first line attack* will re-enter the sector at the last week and will assume the attacking formation during the last days.

The command will take into consideration that at this moment the density of the troops in the forward zone will be increased and it will take the greatest precautions for concealing the assembling and movements of troops. He will organize the marches, transports and supply service which should take place mostly at night.

The divisions assigned for attack in the second line will take their place preserving as long as possible an echelonnement in depth which will allow them to rest their battalions.

Bringing up the infantry rapidly.

179. It will not always be possible to pass through all phases of this procedure.

The following procedure may be used for bringing up the infantry, depending on the time and means that are available.

180. The divisions designated for the second line attack will be the first to enter the sector.

The divisions designated for the first line attack will be assembled in the billets close to the attacking front but where they can nevertheless rest and have facilities for some maneuvers. From these positions they will perform their preparatory reconnaissances. They will put all or part of their staffs, intelligence or liaison services with those of the divisions that are temporarily holding the front.

They will take their place in the first line during the second week as indicated above.

181. It is possible that the first line attacking divisions will be called upon to replace a different number of divisions who have held the front defensively.

The greatest difficulty will arise from the fact that the offensive formation will not coincide with the defensive formation. It will devolve on the army commander to remove this difficulty.

The first line attacking divisions will take their place during the last week and the divisions who have held the sector defensively will constitute the reserves for the army corps or army.

Postponement of the attack.

182. No matter what method of bringing up the infantry has been adopted, the final arrangement should be capable of being modified :

When bad weather or insufficiency of the destructions bring about a postponement of the attack.

When for any reason whatever, the conditions in the plan of engagement must be varied at the last moment.

In this case :

1) The first line attacking divisions make the arrangements and direct their training so that each battalion of each line regiment is prepared for the mission of the first, second, or third line.

When the attack is postponed the interior reliefs are organized so that on the day the attack will be launched the foremost battalions will not have been in the first line more than two days (*).

(*) This will always be possible when the divisions have their three regiments side by side and each regiment its three battalions in depth. It will e only partially possible when the division has two regiments on line (each regiment with two battalions in the first and two in the second line) and one regiment in the third line. This formation is not symmetrical and in case of relief necessitates a circular transfer between the regiments. This is an ad itional reason for placing the regiments side by side.

2) The second line attacking divisions should always be prepared to assume the missions of the first line attacking divisions.

This changing of roles at the last moment is to be avoided. Chances will be more favorable for avoiding it if, within the first line divisions, the command has provided for the transfer of missions and the shifts between battalions.

Verifying the liaison.

183. Verifying the liaison constitutes the most essential task of the command of all echelons during the night and the hours immediately preceding the attack.

The adjustment of watches and the transmission of the time are of utmost importance.

PART III.

EXECUTION.

———

PART III.

EXECUTION.

CHAPTER VIII.

THE ATTACK.

I. — THE IMMEDIATE PREPARATIONS.

184. On the last day of the preparation the command issues the *Order of the attack*, which is usually limited to fixing the hour H (day D) for the debouch of the infantry.

This order must be addressed in writing (*) in order that the first line troops may receive it in time (**); every precaution is taken to insure the *most absolute secrecy*.

185. In order to produce a *surprise* by the debouch of the infantry, the hours preceding the attack must not disclose any unusual activity by the different arms.

These different arms (artillery, anti-aircraft, aeronautics, infantry machine guns) continue and intensify the vigilance which they have been obliged to display during the preparation in order to paralyse the enemy's terrestrial and aerial observation.

186. A) ARTILLERY. — The artillery retains the normal cadence of the preceding days.

(*) In opaque envelope.

(**) Experience proves that at least six hours is required for this order after leaving the command post of the infantry division to arrive in time at the first line.

To this effect, since the hour H must be preceded for several hours by various kinds of fires (neutralization of batteries and observation posts, firing of special shells, concentration fire upon the improvised organizations, time fuse fire upon shell holes), it is important that these fires should not constitute a warning to the enemy. Therefore they must have been repeated every day or at least during the last days of the period of the destruction, under almost analogous conditions but never exactly the same as those of D. This action will add materially to the destruction and the harassment, thus wearing down the opponent both physically and morally.

187. B) The AERONAUTIC SERVICE conforms to the same principle, notably in regard to attacks upon the enemy's aerial service, troops and establishments. The combat and bombing groups must not open this attack, D before H, more violently than on the preceding days. Although it is important that their fighting activity be continued during the last days of the preparation, beginning at the moment when the enemy may surmise the imminence of the attack, it is equally important that it should not reveal the approach of the hour of this attack.

The command and infantry avions do not mingle with the ranging avions unless the proportion of avions in the air is abnormal. They discreetly verify their wireless but do not drop any bombs before H. They should have flown over the lines for several days with their permanent recognition insignia and sent their own wireless indicative or call letter.

It is equally important that the number of balloons sent up should not be abnormally increased during the hours preceding H.

188. C) The INFANTRY concludes its preparations with the greatest order. It utilizes until the last moment the shelters or covers of the parallels of departure and assembly places in order to conceal its density from the enemy's terrestrial or aerial observation posts.

All the elements designated to accompany it (liaison detachments, engineers, territorial units, etc.) take their places under the same conditions.

The *tanks* are kept carefully camouflaged. Any movement or sign which might attract attention to their emplacements must be avoided.

II. — DEBOUCH OF THE ATTACK AND ADVANCE TOWARD THE FIRST INTERMEDIATE OBJECTIVE.

189. The debouch is so planned that the *assaulting troops* may :

1º Cross in one rush the danger zone of the enemy's barrage fire (artillery, machine gun, rifle, bombs or grenades), before this fire is opened (*).

2º Catch the defenders of the enemy's first lines in their trenches and shelters before they have been able to reach their fighting emplacements.

3º Advance toward the first intermediate objective at a rate best adapted to circumstances and to the terrain.

The rate of advance of the infantry must therefore be quite rapid at the departure.

After passing the enemy's first lines it must on the contrary be slow, in order to permit the regular advance of the infantry across the terrain broken up by the bombardment, as well as the steady and methodical advance of the accompanying artillery fire.

The plan of engagement specifies this rate (**) for the different moments between the debouch and the arrival upon the first intermediate objective, then between the

---

(*) Experience has shown that these fires are not opened sooner than 4 or 5 minutes before, when every precaution has been taken to prevent the enemy from learning the exact hour of the attack.

(**) In the determination of the rate, it is necessary to consider the condition and form of the terrain, as well as the obstacles to be crossed; for example, the rate may vary from 100 meters in 1 or 2 minutes at first to 100 meters in 3 or 4 minutes later.

different objectives. The first phase is regulated by a fixed schedule, the first intermediate objective being carefully chosen according to the possibility of the infantry's arriving there without incident.

190. A) The ARTILLERY executes at H its counter-battery, accompanying and protective fire at the rate fixed by the plan of engagement.

a) The **counter-battery fire** continues or intensifies the neutralization begun several hours before.

b) The **accompanying barrage** commences its advance immediately beyond the most advanced parallel of departure, in order to permit the infantry to sally forth and follow closely behind the barrage.

The barrage is advanced by short jumps in order to sweep the entire terrain and form a constant and continuous mask ahead of the infantry.

The accompayning fire is executed principally by field artillery; the creeping barrage, with percussion explosive shells; raking fire by time fuse shells.

c) The **protective barrage** insures during this time a strong protection upon the entire front and flanks of the attack. It must be varied in intensity according to the importance of the points to be swept.

It is executed by a part of the light artillery and by the heavy howitzers, using explosive shells, percussion or time fuse, shrapnel and smoke shells. The effect of explosive shells from the heavy artillery, particularly from rapid fire, is very important from the point of view of morale : it encourages the friendly troops and leads them on, it demoralizes the enemy's troops and causes them to seek shelter.

The counter-attacks are as a rule undertaken in part by the concentration fire of protective groups or batteries.

d) The **advanced reconnaissances of observation are** executed.

191. B) The AERONAUTIC SERVICE departs in full force to maintain and follow up the aerial superiority gained in the preparatory combats.

The bombing and combat groups act in liaison : the former by bombarding continuously the aviation fields, the troops on the march, reserves, batteries, Headquarters, cantonments, etc., the latter by attacking at a low altitude the personnel and everything which they consider vulnerable.

The avions of the command, infantry and artillery, as well as the balloons, carry out their missions of command, observation or ranging.

Some moments after the launching of the attack, when they no longer risk disclosing it, the inf..ntry avions signal with their call rocket, which they set off quite low and slightly in front of their infantry to give them confidence.

192. C) The INFANTRY, with the special detachments designated to accompany it (liaison, engineer, territorial, etc.), masked by the accompanying and protective barrages and sometimes in the rear of mine explosions or tanks which open passages for it, leave the trenches at H and follow close behind the barrage or tanks.

a) The **assaulting troops (first and second line battalions and the battalions at the disposal of the divisional infantry commanders)** advance in open terrain in echelon conforming to the prescribed formation. During the first moments of the attack, the spacing of the units may be reduced in order to permit the maximum number of infantry to pass beyond the danger zone of the enemy's barrages.

The formation advances behind the accompanying barrage; the leading wave presses as closely behind the barrage as possible and crosses the trenches or organizations; the waves echelonned in depth follow the preceding wave and preserve or afterwards assume the mean prescribed distance.

b) The **tactical units assigned to clean up the trenches** descend into the works indicated to them and clean up the trenches, approach trenches, dugouts, command posts, and observation posts.

c) The **reserve troops** advance either in open terrain or by approach trenches.

d) The **machine gun companies**, detailed if necessary for executing indirect long range fire, form the stationary barrages provided for, beyond their infantry.

e) The **units maintaining the lateral liaison** between the battalions, the infantry regiment and the infantry division, advance and form in echelon both in width and in depth in order to insure the constant liaison for which they are responsible.

f) The **units detailed for escorting the prisoners** (*) assemble the prisoners, disarm them and escort them to the rear.

g) The **tactical units detailed to guard the parallels of departure,** previously placed in the rear of the troops of assault, occupy these parallels as soon as they are vacant.

h) The **tactical units detailed to insure provisioning in ammunition and materiel, and to throw forward liaisons or communications**, immediately set to work.

III. — HALTS AT THE INTERMEDIATE OBJECTIVES AND RESUMPTION OF THE ADVANCE.

193. The intermediate objectives are chosen by the command upon lines of the terrain where it will be useful or advantageous to halt momentarily the assaulting troops :

Either to permit them to rest after a long effort.

To re-form and reorganize them before reaching a difficult point in the advance.

Or before the passing of lines.

In any case, to reduce the cadence of the artillery fire, to readjust the barrages and verify the liaisons.

They are assigned by the command (army corps or army) superior to the commanders of the infantry division or chosen by the infantry division commanders.

They should be selected in such a manner as to simplify

(*) Squads or half platoons of territorials or of infantrymen drawn from the reserve units.

the movement of the artillery barrage; it is particularly advantageous that the rate of advance of the infantry should be uniform between two intermediate objectives in order that the rate of displacement of the barrage may also be uniform.

The intermediate objectives are therefore sought for towards the lines of the terrain near which the infantry will be confronted with unfavorable fighting conditions and towards the boundary separating two zones of march for each of which a different rate of advance must be assigned for the infantry.

The length of each halt, roughly estimated, is fixed in the plan of engagement.

194. However we must count upon unfavorable conditions, which necessitate modifications in the schedule, and give the various arms time to adjust it, then to re-form before continuing the advance.

Consequently the plan of engagement for the infantry division includes a *system of alteration of the schedule,* based preferably upon the signal "not ready", displayed at the proper time by the first line troops.

This system must be based upon the following general principles :

1) The alteration of the schedule must provide a sufficient delay to enable the troops to prepare to resume their march. It must also provide a simple plan for determining a new schedule.

An alteration of one hour seems to fulfil these conditions.

2) This alteration should not be determined automatically by direct signals from the infantry to the artillery, for if the first line battalion had the power directly and separately to regulate the accompanying barrage, it might result in a disorganization of the attack.

3) Consequently the usual method will be the fixing of this schedule alteration by the infantry division commander

for the entire front of the infantry division and very exceptionally for only a section of this front (*).

4) The infantry division commander will consider, by weighing the elements of his decision, and by examining the requests which have been addressed to him, the advantage of permitting the attack to continue in order to extricate the delayed battalions by the normal advance of the other battalions.

The infantry division commander gives to the commanders of the neighboring infantry divisions information upon the position of his first lines and the schedule alterations which he has decided upon.

He receives similar information from them.

195. A) The ARTILLERY fixes its accompanying barrage about 200 meters beyond the intermediate objective.

During the halt, it regulates the intensity and rapidity of fire (accompanying, protective and counter-battery) in such a manner as constantly to cover the infantry, protect

---

(*) A good system for the alteration of the schedule established in the plan of engagement may be as follows. The plan establishes :

1) A *normal schedule* containing the time of halts, approximately estimated, upon the intermediate objectives and regulating the development of the attack from beginning to end.

2) The *fixed value for the alteration of the schedule* (for example, 1 hour).

3) A *signal " not ready "*, which the battalions will display during the halt to give notice that they are not ready to resume the advance at the hour specified by the normal shedule.

4) A *signal for the schedule alteration* which the division commander will display during the halt to prescribe the alteration.

Furthermore, in the plan of engagement :

The infantry division commander, if he sees fit, inserts a provision for maneuver and the conditions upon which he purposes to grant or not to grant an alteration of the schedule when it is requested.

He indicates the delays for which the signal "not ready" should be displayed in order that he may decide the alteration and notify the first line in time.

He states whether the alteration of the schedule applies to the entire infantry division or only to the battalion which requested it (in the latter case, which is exceptional, he determines the measures to be taken by the accompanying or protective artillery).

He orders that, whatever may be the requests made, the advance *will be resumed at the hour named in the normal schedule if the signal for the alteration of the schedule has not been given.*

it against counter-attacks and mask the passing of the lines, by employing only the minimum of fire necessary.

The verification of the liaison is provided for.

The batteries will be prepared to resume the creeping barrage (*) at the hour assigned.

If the schedule is altered, the artillery groups acting upon the wings of the infantry division must make all necessary arrangements for coordinating the *delayed barrage* of the infantry division with the *creeping barrage* of the neighboring divisions without interfering with the latter.

Consequently for each intermediate objective the artillery groups acting on the wings should have studied and prepared the solution of this problem.

196. B) The AERONAUTIC SERVICE.

The combat and bombing squadrons continue their offensive action.

The army squadrons reconnoiter the rear of the battle field.

The heavy artillery avions take care of the zones of their groups, and control the fire against the enemy's batteries and bodies of troops.

The command avions observe the general progress of the combat, the reaction of the enemy, the indications of a counter-attack and signal them to the command and to the artillery.

The infantry avions follow and signal the advance of the firing line and of the command posts and maintain the liaison between the command, the infantry and the artillery.

The position of the lines is determined either by time schedule, by lines predetermined by the plan of engagement, or by an order from the infantry division commander transmitted by infantry avion at any moment when it is necessary to specify these emplacements.

(*) It is nearly always impossible to maintain the maximum rate of fire during the halts. It is besides indispensable that at least a part of this halt be employed, to rest the personnel, allow the guns to cool, and bring up ammunition.

197. C) The INFANTRY.

a) **At each halt,** the infantry preserves its echelons in depth, the various waves utilizing the trenches, approach trenches and shell holes or accidents of the terrain.

The officers and N. C. O.'s re-form their units.

They verify all liaisons.

They observe the signals of the infantry avion and either at a predetermined hour, at an indicated line, or upon the request of the avion, they signal the location of the first line (bengal flares, rockets, or location panels), or display the panels of the command post.

They distribute the ammunition, grenades and fireworks which are at hand or which have been brought up by replenishing units.

They specify the mission of the different units, verify the points of direction, designate if necessary new cleaning up units and render all necessary decisions.

They report (whenever possible by sketch) the situation attained.

198. *b)* **During the advance between two intermediate objectives,** the infantry reduces the nests of resistance by its own fire and maneuvers.

It is impossible to obtain the support of the artillery in time for every detailed action, but these *reductions of nests of resistance* will be carried out under cover of the accompanying barrage.

It is to render this cover effective that the average rate of advance is slow and that the infantry division commander chooses the successive intermediate objectives and arranges for a liberal halt upon each.

In this manner, having overcome the obstacle, the infantry may rejoin its barrage and it does not leave the next line of halt until it has been re-formed and reorganized.

199. *c)* **When the halt is made to permit passing of lines,** the first battalions (first line) halt as has been explained in paragraph *a* above.

The second battalions (second line) first halt under the same conditions as the first battalions in order to re-form and prepare their maneuvers. Then, under the conditions stated in the plan of engagement, they advance, led by their officers, the different waves being formed in small columns;—they pass beyond the first battalions, every precaution being taken to avoid confusing and crowding of the effectives;—they deploy, assuming the fighting in the first line;—they continue the advance toward the new objectives *by pressing close behind the shells.*

After this operation, the first battalions assume the mission of the second line, by replacing the second battalions or the mission of the third line by replacing the third battalions (third line); in the latter case they permit the third battalions to pass them when the advance is resumed (*).

200. *d*) The **machine gun groups**, detailed in case of necessity to carry out indirect long range fire, cover the advance of the infantry with stationary barrages.

When the machine gun companies must be moved, they are formed in echelon, advantage being taken of the halts of the troops upon the successive objectives.

The establishment of groups upon the terrain, the plan and schedule of their fire, and their liaisons with the troops and the command must be determined in detail.

201. *e*) The **tanks** continue their advance conformably to their mission of destroying defensive organizations or of accompanying the infantry.

202. *f*) The **units detailed for cleaning up parties, lateral liaison, escorting prisoners, replenishing ammunition and materiel and for reestablishing communications,** execute their mission.

(*) When the distance from the objectives renders it necessary the passing of lines will include the employment of a part of the battalions of the infantry division of the second line. The maneuver of these fourth, fifth,... battalions will then be similar to that described above for the second, third, etc. The rising battalions will pass under the orders of the infantry division commander of the first line and the battalions replaced will be under the orders of the infantry division commander of the 2nd line. The interchanging of the commands of the first and second line in antry divisions will not generally take place before the halt upon the normal objective.

IV. — OCCUPATION OF THE NORMAL OBJECTIVE. — CONSOLIDATION OF CONQUERED TERRAIN. — RECONNAISSANCES. — POSSIBLE OBJECTIVES·

203. As soon as the normal objective is reached, the assaulting troops occupy it, while preserving their echelonment in depth.

The reserve troops halt at their normal distance behind the assaulting units, ready to reinforce or go ahead of them, but until they have to intervene, their officers keep them away from the firing line.

In every unit, the principal care should be to reform and reorganize the troops. This will be the best safeguard both for the conservation of the gains and for their eventual development.

The officers and N. C. O.'s assume the same obligations as for the halt upon an intermediate objective. They comprise the following : the search for observation posts, the verification of liaisons, the communication by signal with the divisional avions and balloons, the replenishing of ammunition and materiel, the determination of the missions devolving upon each unit, the written reports and sketches showing the exact situation.

204. A) The ARTILLERY,

B) The AERONAUTIC SERVICE, } proceed as upon each

C) The INFANTRY,

intermediate objective, except in the following particulars.

The artillery shifts its position as soon as the attack has reached the normal objective.

This is executed in echelon, in order that there may always be a sufficient number of batteries to :

Insure the conservation of the terrain and aid in repulsing counter-attacks.

Continue the preparation upon the subsequent objectives.

205. D) The ORGANIZATION OF THE POSITION is immediately undertaken : each line of battalions sets to work to fortify a parallel (or elements of a parallel). The communications are established and the materiel is brought up by units specially detailed for this purpose.

The officers of all grades apply the previsions of the plan of engagement, supplementing them by any dispositions which the reconnaissance of the terrain may prompt.

In organizing the final position it is advisable to follow the following directions :

It is very important to establish the most advanced parallel at such a distance from the trench to be carried later, that the artillery preparation upon the following objective may be carried out without evacuating the trench or approach trench.

If the assaulting troops have been halted a short distance from a hostile organization which they were unable to capture, only protective elements will remain upon this line : the remainder of the units will fall back to 200 or 300 meters from the enemy's line of resistance, and after re-forming, will immediately begin the future parallel of departure some distance from the artillery preparation.

The protective elements will retire during the night preceding the beginning of the preparation.

The battalion commanders must have this work undertaken under the above conditions without *awaiting an order to this effect*. Thus a good parallel of departure will be prepared along the entire front without useless fatigue to the troops and the preparation for the next attack may be undertaken with the minimum delay.

206. E) The RECONNAISSANCES beyond the normal objective are performed by the designated units or fractions at the hour determined or upon signals prearranged between the infantry and artillery.

They advance under the protection of caging fire from the artillery and machine guns, to reconnoiter the terrain between the normal objective and the possible objective.

It is usually advisable, unless the objectives of these reconnaissances are very few, to launch the reconnaissances simultaneously and to form only a single caging barrage on the entire front of the infantry division.

The mission of some of these reconnaissances is to

destroy the enemy's batteries beyond the normal objective.

They must not attack strongly fortified bodies of the enemy under any circumstances.

Consequently :

If this latter circumstance should occur they gather all the useful information, endeavoring to define the points of the terrain where resistance was encountered and the troops they found there and when their mission is completed, they return to their lines.

If, on the contrary, little resistance is encountered, they advance to the limits of the caging fire and from there launch the signals agreed upon (bengal flares, for informing the avion as to the positions attained,—rockets or other conventional signals, for signaling to terrestrial observation posts,—carrier pigeons, etc.).

207. F) The ADVANCE TOWARDS THE POSSIBLE OBJECTIVE is undertaken, upon observing these signals, under the conditions specified in the plan of engagement.

The infantry units designated advance at the hour or signal agreed upon, and at the prescribed rate of advance.

The artillery covers them by extending its lateral fires progressively, then its frontal caging fire until the possible objective.

This advance toward the possible objective is made by only a part of the assaulting troops (or of the reserve troops).

A large part of the assaulting troops (or reserve troops) continue the occupation and organization of the normal objective.

It is the task of the army commander, at the completion of the attack, to determine what should be the method of occupation of the various objectives in consideration of the results obtained upon the entire front.

Until this decision is known :

The first line division will arrange their line of resistance and line of surveillance according to the local conditions of the terrain, the line of surveillance as a rule being established upon the possible objective.

No advance beyond the possible objective will be undertaken

V. — EXERCISE OF THE COMMAND
IN THE INFANTRY DIVISIONS OF THE FIRST LINE.

208. The above paragraphs, in defining the various phases of the advance, roughly determine the exercise of the command of different echelons.

It is necessary to amplify this in relation to the different arms and to the command of the division.

209. A) ARTILLERY.

During the advance of the infantry, the battalion, group, light artillery and heavy artillery commanders remain at the posts which they have arranged in combat posts and which must overlook as much as possible of the terrain of attack of the infantry which they have to support.

When successive posts have been provided, they will leave a liaison personnel at each post which they quit, in order to insure the permanence of the liaison while they are changing position.

Besides the needs of these liaisons and those of the necessary reserve of the command, the artillery officers and non-commissioned officers have the primary obligation during the course of the attack to insure the liaison with the infantry as far as the first line battalions.

This mission devolves upon liaison detachments, commanded by an officer, made up of a picked personnel and provided with the necessary materiel for keeping the accompanying and protective groups informed upon the situation and the needs of the infantry.

The distribution of these detachments is specified in the plan of liaison.

210. B) AERONAUTIC SERVICE.

The commanders of the squadron and of the balloon company insure the permanence and the continuity of the missions specified in the plan of engagement or of those assigned to them by the infantry division commander in the course of the combat.

As soon as they land the observers report the result of their aerial observation either by telephone or by going in person to the command post of the infantry commander.

It will often be advantageous for the division commander to station an officer from the squadron at his command post during the entire attack.

211. C) INFANTRY.

The *Battalion Commanders* advance at the same time as their units. They take advantage of the halts for approaching the first lines and observing the terrain over which the advance will be continued. At the hours agreed upon, or at these hours increased by the alteration in the schedule (*), they order the advance resumed which presses closely behind the shells. They conform to the prescription of paragraph 3 for the occupation of the normal objectives, the carrying out of reconnaissances, the advance towards the possible objective and the occupation of this objective.

212. The *corps commanders* employ the halts for changing the position of the command posts. They never take up a new command post until the liaison action is insured.

They renew contact with all or part of the battalions, as far as the circumstances of the combat permit it and always insure the permanence of command of their command posts.

They watch carefully the passing of lines.

They hasten the replenishing of ammunition and materiel.

Their primary rôle is to guarantee the direct liaison between their battalions and the artillery which supports them. They employ for this purpose the *artillery liaison detachments and their own telephone, wireless telegraph, earth induction and visual signalling parties* in order to be always in direct communication with the accompanying and protective artillery and with the command. They complete this liaison by *chains of couriers.*

(*) If the schedule is adjusted, the battalion commander makes the necessary corrections in the table of march schedules with the greatest care.

They send (or cause to be sent by the first line battalions) written information by *carrier pigeons* and by runners. They repeat, conforming to the plan of liaison, all or part of the signals displayed by the first lines.

They insure the execution of previsions of the plan of engagement for the operations between the normal and possible objective. They issue the necessary orders for the occupation and organization of these objectives and the echelonnement of the battalions.

213. The *divisional infantry commanders* proceed like the corps commanders, allowance being made for the difference in units; thanks to the successive positions of well chosen and well prepared command posts, they follow closely the assaulting troops which they command (*). Their rôle in the combat consists in controlling the execution of the plan of engagement, principally for the passing of lines, and in regulating the entrance into action of the battalions immediately at hand and those which the infantry division commander places at their disposal during the course of the combat. They are constantly preoccupied with the functioning of the liaison between the infantry and the artillery and between the infantry and the infantry division, and request from the infantry division commander the necessary means for improving it. They observe and follow the progress of the combat, especially during the advance toward the possible

(*) Chapter II, paragraph 38, lays down the principle that the assaulting troops are under the command of the divisional infantry commanders. In the infantry divisions, with three regiments, attacking upon a narrow front (for instance, the infantry division formed *in a square* with 3 battalions in line and 3 lines of battalions in depth), this rôle will not offer particular difficulties for the divisional infantry commanders.

In the infantry divisions of three regiments attacking upon an extended front (for instance 4 or 5 battalions in line) the front will be too great and the depth too small for the divisional infantry commander to effectively command the whole of the assaulting troops. In this case the infantry division commander assigns him the command of the most important part. The other part may be under the orders of a corps commander who is directly responsible to the infantry division commander.

In exceptional cases the divisional infantry commander may receive the command of such a group of assaulting or reserve troops, which will be made up according to circumstances.

objective, and address to the infantry division commander, reports-from which the elements of important decisions by the command will often be drawn.

214. D) TELEGRAPH SERVICE.

The officers and non-commissioned officers of the telegraphic detachments, during the entire attack and as soon as the objectives are attained, have the following rôle :

To insure the operation of the posts.

To extend the communications and to establish new posts according to the plan of liaison.

These works are so important and so difficult that it will always be necessary, in the division, for the chief of Staff to assume in person the direction of the telegraph service and of the liaison.

There must be cooperation and direct liaison between the advanced observation of the artillery and the telegraphic service which must render them special assistance beginning with H.

215. D) ENGINEERS.

During the course of the advance and at its completion, the engineer commander in each infantry division either executes reconnaissances of the terrain or orders them executed with a view to :

Insuring the special missions which may devolve upon certain fractions marching with the assaulting troops or detailed to execute special work for their benefit.

Fulfilling the principal mission of the engineers in this phase of the battle which consists in reestablishing communications and bringing up materiel.

He organizes and details to this effect the working units placed at his disposal.

The mission of the engineer officers is :

To advance their units under the conditions laid down in the plan of engagement.

To carry out the reconnaissances which are assigned to them.

To superintend the work of their units and of those which are detailed for reestablishing communications.

216. E) The INFANTRY DIVISION COMMANDER remains during the action at his command post, which is the point of arrival of all terrestrial or aerial information.

He may not be called upon to render important decisions in the course of the combat if the latter progresses favorably and conformably to the plan of engagement : hence he follows from this the different phases and insures the constant support of the infantry by the artillery.

To this purpose he communicates by regulation signals with the infantry avion and orders the squadron commander to dispatch a new avion if there is a situation to be specified or a special mission to be fulfilled.

He takes care that the reserve battalions are employed and pushed forward according to the plan of engagement. He endeavors to hold them available until the end of the attack and if necessary he assigns their mission in case impending counter-attacks are observed.

When unfavorable cirumstances compel him to call upon his reserves he endeavors to use them to the best advantage.

If the condition of the communications permit, he is advised upon this subject by the divisonal infantry commander and by the reports of the staff liaison officers or aerial observers.

When the objectives have been attained he definitely determines with the divisional artillery commander all the measures to be taken for their conservation; these measures having already been outlined in the plan of engagement;

The system to be adopted for the barrage fires which must continue to protect the infantry during the evening and night after the attack;

Organization of the counter-preparation and counter-attack barrages;

Continuation of the preparation, if new attacks have been provided for in the plan of engagement or if the objectives have not been entirely attained.

Changing the position of the batteries.

If the objectives have not been entirely attained, the infantry division commander orders the reconnaissances carried out immediately after the combat.

After examining the situation, he draws up a summary plan with a view to the liquidation of the operation. He submits an outline of this to the commander of the army corps and upon his approval, he issues the orders of execution.

If the objectives have been completely occupied, he learns definitely by every means, particularly by the aviation, the situation and the reconnaissances of the troops which have attained the possible objective.

He reports to the commander of the army corps : upon the conditions more or less favorable to the development of the success;

Upon the possibility of continuing the operation with his own troops;

Upon the necessity of *relieving* (*) or passing his division by a second line division.

(For the development of the success see chapter IX.)

The successive changing of position of the command posts of the infantry division is carried out according to the directions in chapter II, paragraph 41.

VI. — EXERCISE OF THE COMMAND IN THE FIRST AND SECOND LINE.
THE ARMY CORPS AND THE ARMY.

217. A) The COMMANDERS OF THE SECOND LINE INFANTRY DIVISIONS insure their advance in the wake of the first line divisions in conformity with the plan of engagement of the army corps.

(*) It is evident as has been explained in the note on page 135 that to reach its normal or possible objective, a first line division must have the support of a certain number of battalions of the second line division corresponding to it, by interchanging with the battalions of the first line division; the passing (or the relieving) will consist in the liberation of the first line division and in the interchanging of the commands.

They take the measures necessary to diminish the losses and to guarantee the freedom of the movements (approaches, distances, formations, etc...).

The commanders of all units move, in conformity with the principles stated in chapter II, in such a manner as to always be in touch with the situation and in liaison with the corresponding officers of the leading division.

The artillery (personnel and materiel) of the second line infantry division usually precede the infantry; it is employed, wholly or in part, in the preparation or in the accompaniment of the attack and the use of its batteries is specified in the plan for changing the position of the army corps artillery (or in that of the first line division, if the artillery of the second line division has been placed under its orders).

Each second line division should be prepared on the evening of the attack, to replace the corresponding first line division.

This will be a passing if the attack is merely suspended and if the operations are resumed immediately afterwards with an interchanging of rôle between the two divisions.

It will be a *relief* if the attacks are not immediately resumed and if the first line division after its replacement does not remain as a direct support to the division which replaced it.

With skilled officers who have effected all their reconnaissances during the combat such an operation may be completed in a single night.

This is one of the conditions essential to the rapidity of succession of the attacks.

218. B) The ARMY CORPS COMMANDERS endeavor :

To maintain close liaison with their first line divisions in order to coordinate their efforts and to efficiently employ the corps artillery to their advantage.

To regulate the advance and engagement of their reserve units.

The mission of the reserve units can not be improvised

upon the terrain.   It is indicated in the plan of engagement in conditional form.

It is confirmed or modified, if necessary, during the action : therefore the army corps commanders must form a clear idea of the situation and render their decisions without delay, because of the slowness of movements upon the battle field.

The work of the army corps commanders does not cease from the moment their reserve units receive the order to enter the action; they superintend their movements, hastening them or rectifying them as necessary. They are responsible for their arrival at the scene of action at the desired time.

When the line of combat is checked by the enemy's organization, thus necessitating a new artillery preparation, the army corps commanders confirm or modify the plan of engagement upon the subject of the resumption of the preparation according to the replacements or reliefs to be executed. They establish summarily a new plan of engagement, altering if necessary the sectors of engagement of the large units, of the heavy artillery, enter into liaison with the neighboring army corps to insure the coordination of efforts and as soon as they have received the approval of the army commander, give the orders of execution.

When all the objectives have been attained, the army corps commanders study the situation from the whole of the reports, especially those of the aviation; they determine the possibilities for the development of the success, halt their arrangements in this direction, to report to the army commander and upon his approval execute it without delay (see chapter IX).

The army corps commanders direct particular attention to the struggle against the enemy's artillery which they direct through the corps artillery commander.

When the attack is launched, the enemy will generally bring into action a large number of batteries, which have not yet been revealed; it will be the rôle of the army corps commanders to assign these batteries as objectives to the groups or battalions which will have been reserved for this purpose; and to have the necessary concentration fire directed upon them.

219. C) The ARMY COMMANDER watches the progress of the action from the reports of the army corps commanders, the staff liaison officers and of the aviation.

He coordinates the action of the army corps artillery and modifies if necessary the missions of the army artillery group.

He regulates the use of the large reserve units of the army.

He studies and combines the plans which are submitted to him by the army corps commanders for continuing or developing the success and decides whether these operations will be executed upon the initiative of the army corps commanders or will give rise to a new general action.

As soon as possibilities arise for the development of the success, he determines from them the conditions of its execution.

CHAPTER IX.

DEVELOPMENT OF THE SUCCESS.

220. An army which has been assigned a mission of offensive action may have to continue its attacks after the first success, if it still possesses available means or if new means are assigned to it.

In anticipation of this emergency, *a general plan for subsequent attacks and for the development of the success* is inserted in the plan of action of the Army and in the plan of engagement for the army corps and infantry division (paragraph II *e*) of Plan of action or Plan of engagement).

Such a plan can contain detailed previsions only so far as the results of the first attacks are concerned; the subsequent operations will be an exact function of the success of the first attack, of the maintenance of the combat by a system of passings or reliefs, and of the *pushing forward of communications, liaisons, and provisioning of all kinds.*

In brief : *every offensive action well launched and resolutely carried out may bring about a maneuver for widening the front of attack.* In the course of this maneuver, the methods of combat may be found to be identical with the methods of attack against fortified positions.

The large units will conform to this governing idea for the moral preparation of their troops and for the special training for the offensive.

I. — CONDITIONS FOR RESUMING THE ADVANCE BEYOND THE POSSIBLE OBJECTIVES.

221. The plans of action and of engagement for an attack specify :

That any advance beyond the possible objective is forbidden unless a decision to this effect is reached by the Army Commander.

Consequently :

The *Army Commander* determines the conditions for the development of the success from the reports made by the commanders of the army corps engaged and from the reconnaissances which he has had carried out during the course of the combat.

As a rule, he orders the following up of the attack only if the success has been obtained on a wide enough front to permit the continuation of the attack with several divisions side by side.

He plans his maneuver in such a manner as to release and push forward the large units which might have been delayed in order that the operations for widening the breach may be executed upon a wide front and with the maximum number of divisions possible.

He seeks to use all or part of his reserves to increase the lateral pressure and thus disengage the neighboring armies.

His decisions are carried to the large units concerned, *by the most rapid means,* under the *form of an order of operations* which confirms, modifies or completes the plan of developemnt of the success and fixes definitely the time for renewing the advance.

The *Generals commanding the large units* (Army Corps, Cavalry Corps, Infantry Divisions, Cavalry Divisions), issue their own *orders of operations*.

These orders of operations to the various echelons must have in general a context similar to that which has been fixed in chapter V, paragraph XII, Plans of action and of engagement.

They report to the supreme commander *that any advance would be useless and dangerous, if the artillery, the ammunition and supplies of all kinds could not follow* and they provide in detail for the reestablishing of communications and liaison.

They detail for this latter mission strong effectives which may be drawn from the large units of the second line or of the reserve.

II. — MECHANISM OF THE DEVELOPMENT OF THE ADVANCE OVER ORGANIZED POSITIONS.

222. At first, the advance will be developed over organized positions, over wrecked and difficult terrain, with the constant prospect of seeing the enemy's defenses break into action again. Therefore the advance will be cautious and methodical.

The advance, always subject to the decisions of the Army Commander will be undertaken either by the infantry divisions which have led the attack in the first line or by the infantry divisions of the second line.

223. The **infantry divisions which have led the attack in the first line** should as a rule be called upon only to start the resumption of the advance.

It is well, even if these divisions are not entirely depleted, to detail them preferably for the organization and occupation of the conquered position between the normal objective and the possible objective.

If they have to start the resumption of the advance, they will carry it out by detachments which having previousyl chosen their points of direction will advance under the conditions specified in the order of operations.

These detachments by a signal agreed upon will cause a covering artillery fire to advance ahead of them.

They will march either in skirmish line or in lines of small columns, followed by cleaning up parties who search the covers.

They will not advance beyond a limit which has been assigned and will establish themselves in surveillance formation amply echeloned in front as well as in depth.

224. The **second line divisions,** by their reconnaissances in the course of the combat, must always be prepared to assume the mission of the first line divisions and also the development of this mission.

Under the conditions stated in the order of operations, they will pass the first line divisions : they will advance by successive rushes, employing formations and methods similar to those used by the first line division in their march toward their normal and possible objectives.

225. The assignment of liaison transversals is recommended.

The command will generally assign a certain number which should not be exceeded without authorization by him.

In the course of this phase :

If the enemy is so disorganized that the divisions are able to advance without encountering great resistance, their batteries will follow the infantry by successive displacemnets, ready to furnish it instantaneous support.

If the enemy resists, it will not be necessary to follow him but to attack him by the established method.

226. A) The ARTILLERY will be prepared to cover all the most advanced elements.

There will be no question of assuring barrage as in the

course of the advance toward the normal and possible objectives, and the real protection for the advance will consist in disorganizing the enemy and capturing the batteries.

The elements will be covered by the cooperation of the field batteries, which at the beginning of the attack will be concealed in line with the parallels of departure, the long range batteries of short guns, and the batteries of long guns which can at this time be placed at the disposal of the divisions.

The disorganization of the enemy will permit more boldness in the bringing up of certain batteries, especially during maneuvers of passing (*).

227. B) The AERONAUTIC SERVICE will be more active as the difficulties in the use of artillery increase.

The fighting and bombing squadrons may render effective service against a disorganized and demoralized enemy, with machine guns, light guns and bombs.

The command, infantry and artillery avions will continue their mission of observation, control, accompanying the infantry, and possibly of transmitting the orders of the command by signal.

228. C) The INFANTRY, as the progression is achieved and the disorganization of the enemy becomes greater, will abandon its march formations and will assume one of greater depth.

The units withdrawn from the advance formation will cooperate in reestablishment of communications and liaison as well as in bringing up supplies.

The *tanks* will at this time have the greatest utility, in accompanying the infantry and furnishing constant support with its mobile and protected artillery. Special provisions will be made to insure their replenishment.

(*) The infantry division commander, by means of the divisional artillery commander, remains in command of all the divisional artillery; this arrangement is particularly important at a time when any premature attempt at decentralization would incur the risk of congesting the approaches and communications.

229. D) The ENGINEERS will rapidly continue the reestablishment of communications.

230. E) The CAVALRY will resume its place in the battle when the field is opened to the initiative and the maneuver of large units and when it will be necessary to precede them in order to preserve the contact.

The divisional cavalry will at first debouch by small fractions, patrols or platoons; later the large cavalry units will draw near the large infantry units, ready to pass them.

The army commander and under him the commanders of the large units will issue their orders for crossing open terrain, reconnoitering the positions to which the enemy has fallen back, and for the attack and investment of these new positions.

The cavalry must then be provided with its own aviation which on the one hand will precede, control and prolong its action; on the other will maintain, by weighted messages, landing or wireless, a direct liaison with the friendly troops and the command.

III. — DEVELOPMENT OF THE ADVANCE IN OPEN TERRAIN.

231. The essential principle of these successive maneuvers is that *the contact must never be lost;* it is a question not only of following the enemy but of closely pursuing him when he attemps to get away, by profiting by the advantages which his still intact system of communications and liaisons afford.

Hence the command may be led to adopt march formations more and more open and flexible, in which the rôle of the different arms will be characterized as follows :

232. A) The ARTILLERY will continue as long as possible to advance by echelons from position to position in such a manner as to be able constantly to support the most advanced infantry fractions.

This will be carried out in columns when aerial and cavalry information will justify it.

At this time, certain long range materiel will be brought up to the head of the column.

The artillery of the cavalry division which it will often be found advantageous to reinforce, will be employed according to the same principles, with still more rapidity and flexibility.

The commanders of the large units will be able to place artillery fractions under the direct order of a commander of the advance guard or of a detachment of all arms.

233. B) The AERONAUTIC SERVICE will reconnoiter and harass the retreating columns, bombard the communications and depots, and pursue the enemies aerial patrols.

Its principal mission will consist in discovering and photographing the halting line where the enemy will organize his resistance and delivering this information to the cavalry corps or divisions and to the commander of the large units of all echelons.

It should have liaison agents at the intelligence centers of the infantry divisions ready to receive the missions which the infantry division commanders will give to the squadrons at their disposal.

Landing grounds will be sought for as near as possible to the intelligence centers. If none can be found, the telephonic liaison, the wireless and the automobile liaison between the intelligence centers and the aviation grounds will insure the rapid transmission of orders.

The avions will very often make use of weighted messages for transmitting information to all the echelons of the command. They will descend when possible close to the troops and command post.

As soon as the advance has been sufficient, the observers, the commander of the army corps avions and a photographic detachment will move to the advanced grounds, leaving only the avions, the pilots, the photographic section and a limited number of officers at the normal landing grounds.

234. C) The INFANTRY will abandon more and more its march formations as soon as the advance is no longer a succession and chain of attacks.

The first step will be to diminish the density of its front and to adapt it to the communications available.

Thus an army corps in square formation will usually not be able to advance more than one of its divisions in the zone of action which had been assigned to it. Often it will even be necessary to join two zones of attack of the army corps in order to have a passage for the infantry division.

It devolves upon the command to group or transport to the rear the unemployed divisions.

Each infantry division in the advance will be echeloned in depth; at first in a semi-deployed formation for crossing fields until aerial or cavalry information will indicate an approaching engagement;—then in one or several columns in route formation.

235. D) The ENGINEERS will facilitate the advance of the infantry by destroying obstacles and by insuring means of passage. It will continue the reestablishment of communications.

236. E) The CAVALRY will maintain the contact.

The army cavalry (army corps or cavalry division) will be directed according to the information concerning the enemy and the terrain furnished by the aviation and the divisional cavalry; its mission will be to search and harass by its fire the retreating columns, to prevent the arrival of reinforcements, to overcome by flanking them the localized resistance with which the enemy might attempt to check the pursuit, to reconnoiter by dismounted and artillery action the halting lines which it will be unable to flank.

The command, in assigning a definite mission to the cavalry should make sure that it will arrange the necessary means of action and will be able to bring them to the scene of action (cavalry, artillery, aviation, foot regiment, cyclists, means of transport, artillery ammunition, supplies).

237. Liaisons. — The staff, infantry division, and army corps commanders, will insure the liaison by their diligence.

The *axis of liaison* for each infantry division will be formed by the line of advance of the principal column.

The telegraph detachment of the infantry division accompanied by the necessary conveyances will march with the leading elements of this principal column. It may be reinforced by the units of telegraph linemen of the army corps. Its mission will be to string the wire upon the axis of liaison and to install the successive relays provided for, upon which the corps or artillery battalions advancing outside of the liaison axis (*) may branch.

The relays best situated for observing the terrain of the advance will be utilized as *intelligence centers*. The infantry division commander will move from center to center by the most rapid means. The permanency of the staff will be insured at the rear center unless the infantry division commander has not arrived at the advanced center (**).

The center where the orders and information of all descriptions should arrive will be distinguished by special panels or flags.

. The rear centers, upon being released by the division, will be taken over by the army corps telegraph service.

The axis of liaison of the army corps will be that of its first line infantry division (or of one of its first line divisions).

IV. — RECONNAISSANCE AND ATTACK UPON THE POSITIONS PREPARED FOR CHECKING THE PURSUIT.

The command in communication with the aviation and cavalry will always be prepared to reconnoiter and to attack

---

(*) The lateral branchings will be carried out only at the approach of a combat.

(**) Consequently the chief of staff must organize double crews to carry on the service of the centers.

the positions prepared by the enemy for checking the pursuit.

238.   A) THE ARTILLERY. — When the columns have before them a sufficient screen of cavalry, a part of the artillery may precede the infantry to support the reconnaissance service of the cavalry.

In every case, the artillery will prepare its entrance into action in order to be in a position to support the infantry as soon as the latter is engaged.

239.   B) The AERONAUTIC SERVICE will verify its previous information.

The avions and balloons will notify the battalions or batteries ready for fire.   They will verify the ranges.

240.   C) The INFANTRY will extend its formations and will choose its approaches in such a manner as to prevent being taken by surprise by gun fire when in column of route formation.

Whether it is preceded by the cavalry and artillery or not, it will advance towards the resisting positions by utilizing the terrain and as soon as it arrives in contact with the first hostile elements, it will test their strength by engaging them; it will attack the advance posts, establishing itself in such a manner as to cover its artillery and hold the observation posts.

During these preliminary operations in which the first line battalions should never risk useless losses, the main body of the infantry will form in echelon in preparation to attack : *the real attack should be carried out only after preparation.*

241.   D) The ENGINEERS will engage in the reconnaissances and in work of organization of the terrain in preparation for the execution of the attack.

242.   E) The CAVALRY will permit the infantry to pass it and will furnish any information obtained during the reconnoitering combat in which it will have already engaged.

243. The conditions of the attack will then be governed by the *orders of engagement* of the commanders of the large units.

Whatever may be the circumstances these orders will be drawn from the principles which are the foundation of the present instruction :

1) In any offensive action, never risk the infantry against organized points without having prepared the attack.

2) In any defensive action, hold the front with a minimum of forces. but use the maximum number of guns at the disposal of the infantry.

3) Economize the infantry, abolish all dense formations.

4) Insure a close liaison between the different arms, even if the action must be retarded.

G. H. Q., October 31, 1917.
PÉTAIN.

SUPPLEMENTS

SUPPLEMENT I.

SKETCHES AND TABLES TO BE USED IN CONNECTION WITH THE PLANS FOR THE EMPLOYMENT OF ARTILLERY.

244. Plans for the Employment of Artillery are drawn up in conformity with the ideas expressed in the second part.

This appendix gives examples or models of the sketches, tracings and tables which should be made use of under the different headings of the Plan of Employment of the Artillery whenever such forms can be used.

I. — SKETCHES.

245. A) Sketch, scale of 1/10000 giving the assignment of all troops on the day D and at the hour H.

This sketch will be got up by the Division (G. S. of D.). It is of particular interest to the Artillery in relation to its liaison organization. It should show the distribution, not only of the battalions, but of the companies, of the first line.

246. B) Sketch, scale of 1/20000, showing the location of the divisional artillery, the command posts, the observation posts and the zones of normal action.

A sheet attached to this sketch will show the telephone communications (in black) and the visual communications (in red).

This sketch will be got up by the Division (G. S. of D. A.).

247. C) Sketch, scale of 1/5000 showing destructive work to be done by the trench artillery and the heavy howitzers.

A sheet attached to this sketch will show the destructive work to be done by the light artillery.

This sketch will be got up by the division (G. S. of D. A.). and will show :

a) In **red**, that which has to do with the 75 mm. guns.

(For the wire entanglements, mark exactly the cuts to be made, in order that one may be able to judge exactly the number, direction and size of the breaches which each battalion should find in front of it.)

b) In **yellow**, that which has to do with the trench artillery.

c) In **blue**, that which has to do with 155 mm. howitzers.

(If the occasion should arise in which it is necessary to make breaches in a trench which the infantry must cross, indicate exactly the location and the number of breaches).

d) In **green**, that which has to do with the 220 mm. mortars.

e) In **black**, that which has to do with all other calibers.

Alongside of each objective (breaches, supporting points and systems of communication to be destroyed, etc.) place a number which will show the number of shots which should be fired to accomplish the work.

248. D) Sketch, scale of 1/10000, showing the movement of the artillery fire in the accompaniment of the infantry during the attack and the dispositions made for protective fire.

The sketch D will be got up by the Division (G. S. of D. A.) and will show :

a) The method of initial fire.

b) The method of fire for the intermediate objectives.

c) The method of limited fire which assures the protection of the infantry after the carrying of the normal (or possible) objective.

This work will be done separately for the field artillery (sketch D-1) and for the heavy artillery (sketch D-2.)

249. .E) Sketch, scale of 1/20000, showing the method of employment of the counter batteries on the day of the attack (neutralization plan).

This sketch will be got up by the corps (G. S. of artillery).

In order to reduce work the number of copies reproduced will be limited to those strictly necessary and the work will not be commenced until after approval by higher authority.

II. — TRACINGS.

250. To the table of terrestrial observation stations should be attached a tracing made up in accordance with the method indicated on page 248 of the *Manuel de l'officier orienteur*, and showing for each square of the tracing the observation posts having a view of the corresponding parts of the terrain.

III. — TABLES.

251. The methods for making the regulation tables are given below.

IV. — METHOD OF ENUMERATING HEAVY BATTERIES AND THE CONVENTIONAL SIGNS.

252. A) ENUMERATION.

In each army, the emplacements for the heavy batteries are numbered beginning with 1, from the west to the east or from the south to the north. In order to avoid too frequent changes in the numbers, newly created battery emplacements receive numbers such as 3', 4'', 3''', etc.

A battery which occupies an emplacement already numbered takes the number of that emplacement, whatever its caliber may be.

The number of a battery is followed by one of the letters A, T or P, according to whether the battery is hauled by animals, by tractors, or is a battery of position.

253. B) TABLE OF CONVENTIONAL SIGNS FOR REPRESENTING ON THE MAP, BATTERIES, DEPOTS AND PARKS.

The arrows are directed toward the middle of the fields of fire.

PIECES.	EMPLACEMENTS.	PIECES.	EMPLACEMENTS.
Battery of 95. .		Battery of 155 C. .	155 C Ch 155 CS
— 105. .		— 220 . . .	220 S
— 120. .		— 8 in. . .	
— 155. .	155 LS 145 155 155 GPF	— 270 . . .	siège côte
— 14, 16, 19.	1 ● 4	— 280 . . .	
— 24, 240.	2 ● 4 Trucs 1 ● 9	— 370 mortar.	
— 27, 285.		— 370 howitzer.	
— 32, 305, 340.	3 ◆ 2 240 CH	— 400 howitzer.	
— 58 trench.		Anti-aircraft artillery	
— 150 trench.		Captive balloon . .	
— 240 trench.		Observation post. .	
		Intermediate depot.	D P I
		Park	▭ P

Explanation :

LS. — Long Schneider.
DPF. — Filloux gun.
CH. — Saint-Chamond.
C Ch. — Short Saint-Chamond.
CS. — Short Schneider.

S. — Schneider.
Siege. — Siege gun.
Côte. — Coast.
Trucs. — Truck mount.
C. — Short.

a) The lozenge represents heavy railroad artillery.

b) Unoccupied emplacements are shown by the same symbol as the material therefor, but the central square, circle or lozenge is left white.

TABLE I.

ARTILLERY ORGANIZATION

of the   Army.

of the   Army Corps.

of the   Division.

Command Post   *Date.*

GROUPS Comdr.	BATTALIONS Comdr.	PARTS at the disposal of the Infantry.	BATTERIES.	CALIBERS.	LOCATION of command Posts.	OBSERVATION Posts.	CALL letters.	REMARKS.
North Grou-ping.		. .			3413	3414	LA	
Colonel.	II/283. Major.	Zone of 1st Bn. 30th Inf.	4/283 5/283 6/283	155 C. S.	4554 4659 4661 4764	5088 5441 5560 5620	LM	
	IV/286. Major.	Zone of 2nd Bn. 30th Inf.						

T<small>ABLE</small> II.

DESTRUCTION OF HOSTILE BATTERIES

by the artillery of the   Army.
of the   Army Corps.

Command Post . *Date.*

GROUPS.	BATTALIONS or batteries.	HOSTILE batteries.	ORDER of relative urgency for destruction.	REMARKS.

TABLE II (*a*).

RECORD OF DESTRUCTION
FIRE ON HOSTILE BATTERIES

carried out by the artillery of the   Army.
of the   Army Corps.

Command Post   *Date.*

GROUPS of H. A.	HOSTILE batteries in the normal zone.	CALIBER.	JULY			
			1	2	3	4
	44.56	77	*	*	*	* 155c 500
	44.59	105			*	
Group A.	45.61	15		*		
	45.67	21	*	* 155c 400		
	46.50	77	*			
	49.62	m. c.	*			
	49.64	105	*	*		
Group B.	51.60	15		*	* 155c 400	

(*) Located in action.

155c / 400   Objective of a destruction fire with the notation of the caliber employed and the number of shots fired.

TABLE III.

ARTILLERY NEUTRALIZATION

by the artillery of the   Army.

of the   Army Corps.

Command Post   *Date.*

GROUPS.	BATTALIONS or batteries.	HOSTILE BATTERIES		REMARKS.
		In the normal zone.	In the possible zone.	

TABLE IV.

DESTRUCTION OF OBSERVATION POSTS, COMMUNICATIONS AND ORGANIZED POINTS

by the artillery of the   Army.

of the   Army corps.

OR DESTRUCTIVE WORK

by the artillery of the   Division.

Command Post   *Date.*

GROUPS	BATTALIONS and batteries.	OBJECTIVES assignad to each battalion (*).	NUMBER of shots allowed for the destruction of each objective.	ORDER in which the targets should be attacked.	MEANS of observation placed at the disposition of each battalion	REMARKS (**).

(*) The objectives should be indicated in a very precise and detailed manner for the guns of the more important calibres.

(**) Bring out very plainly the methods followed to prevent repairs to destructions already made.

TABLE V.

HARASSING AND PROHIBITIVE FIRE ON ENEMY COMMUNICATIONS AND ORGANIZED POINTS

by artillery of the   Army.

of the   Army Corps.

of the   Division.

During the period from   to

Command Post   *Date.*

GROUPS	BATTALIONS and batteries.	OBJECTIVES to be attacked.	NUMERICAL order.	DAILY allowance.	GENERAL indication of the way in which the fire should be conducted.	REMARKS.

NOTE. Table V allows for a certain amount of firing from which is chosen each day the amount to be used for prohibitive fire.

Table V is modified and kept up to date in accordance with all information received from the air service, observation posts, prisoners, etc.

TABLE VI.

FIRE AGAINST TRANSIENT OBJECTIVES

by the artillery of the   Army.
            of the   Army Corps.
            of the   Division.

Command Post   *Date.*

GROUPS.	DESIG-NATED batteries.	CORRESPOND-ING wireless call letter.	ZONE of action.	OBSER-VATION posts.	BALLOONS.	REMARKS.

TABLE VII.

TABLE OF CONCENTRATION

of the artillery of the   Army Corps.

Command Post   *Date.*

OBJECTIVES.	REGULATING observation posts.	BATTALIONS or batteries.	GROUPS.	REMARKS.

NOTE. Got up according to the methods prescribed in Chapter XIV, *Manuel de l'Officier Orienteur.*

TABLE VIII.

ARTILLERY MOVEMENTS.

Counter-Batteries of the   Army.
            of the   Army Corps.
Destruction Batteries of the   Division.

Command Post   *Date.*

GROUPS.	BATTALIONS and batteries.	NEW emplace-ments.	NEW observation posts.	PROBABLE dates of movement.	REMARKS (*).

(*) Particularly the personnel detailed to perform certain labor, such as preparing roads and trench crossings, etc.

NOTE. The Movement Table is kept constantly up to date during the battle.

TABLE IX.

ESTIMATE OF AMMUNITION (*)
NECESSARY UP TO AND INCLUDING THE DAY D.

IX. **Field Artillery.**

Rounds of Shrapnel.
Rounds of High Explosives Shell, Normal Charge.
Rounds of High Explosive Shell, Reduced Charge,
Fuses A. R. (delayed action), I (Instantaneous).
S. R. (non-delayed action), I. A. (long instantaneous), D. E. (combination).

IXª. **Heavy Artillery** (for each calibre).

Shell.
Charges.
Fuses.
Primers.

IXᵇ. **Trench Artillery** (for each calibre).

Bombs.
Charges.
Primers.

IXᶜ. **Gas Shells.**

(*) Each calibre is kept in a separate column.

TABLE X.

FIRING DAYS

By "firing day" is meant the mean amount of ammunition which it necessary to provide for each piece for a certain operation (several days of preparation and the execution).

The following table gives the firing days for the light artillery and the heavy artillery.

For the 75 mm. guns . . . . 300 rounds.

HEAVY GUNS.		HEAVY HOWITZERS.	
95	150 rds.	155 Mod. 1912 . . .	120 rds.
105	150 "	155 C. Ch.	150 "
120	120 "	155 C. S.	
155 Mod. 77. . . .	100 "	220	80 "
155 G. P. F.		220 T. R.	100 "
145-155	120 "	8"	
155 L. S.		270 S.	50 "
		280	60 "

The allowances for the trench artillery depend on the destructive work to be done. The following table gives for each class the maxima that one should demand of a mortar for one day's firing (*).

58	150 rds.
75	300 "
150	150 "
240	60 "

(*) The above amounts for daily fire cannot, however, be attained if the mortars are not on platforms and the personnel which serves them is not reinforced. In this connection it may be better not to put all the batteries of the divisional artillery in action at one time or even all the mortars of one battery. By doing this one has at his disposal the necessary reinforcements for labor, resupply, and for reliefs for the cannoneers.

SUPPLEMENT II.

INFORMATION ABOUT ARTILLERY FIRE.

254. The following numbers are understood to refer to well executed and well observed fire.

I. — DESTRUCTION OF THE HOSTILE ARTILLERY.

255. A) CALIBRES TO BE EMPLOYED ACCORDING TO THE AMOUNT TO WHICH THE BATTERY TO BE DESTROYED IS PROTECTED.

Unprotected batteries : 75, 105, 120 (F. A. shell), 145 (F. A. shell), 155 (F. A. shell).

Slightly protected batteries : 120 (long shell), 145 (high explosive shell, Mod. 16), 155 (F. A. shell, Mod. B. shell).

Medium protected batteries (emplacements not concrete covered) (*) : 155 (long shell), 16, 19.

Strongly protected batteries (concrete covered emplacements) (*) : 220, 270, 280, 293, 370, 24, 240, 27, 285, 32.

256. B) MEAN EXPENDITURE OF AMMUNITION NECESSARY FOR THE ASSURED DESTRUCTION OF BATTERIES.

The number of projectiles necessary for the destruction of a certain battery is directly proportional to the value of the probable error of the guns used; it varies with the material used and the range.

In principle, if the probable error is greater than 50 meters there is no use in attempting destruction.

(*) Against artillery in casemates the 75 mm. gun can do very efficient work in firing at the embrasures up to about 5000 meters. Under normal circumstances in attacking casemates, the number of rounds to be fired in order to get two direct hits on the target is 100 at a range of 3000 meters and 200 rounds at a range of 5000 meters, giving as a mean about 150 rounds which must be fired for each hostile piece to be destroyed.

The mean expenditure to be expected is as follows :

75	500 to 800 rounds according to range.
120 145 155 L	400 to 600 rounds according to range.
155 C	300 to 400 rounds according to range.
16 19 220 240	200 to 300 rounds according to range.
27 270 280 285 293	150 to 200 rounds according to range.
32 370	About 100 rounds.

257. C) Fire for the destruction of a nest of batteries.

Concentrated fire against nests of batteries is generally more effective :

If it is executed with the largest calibres or the pieces having the longest range, which will permit of oblique fire.

If the fire bursts forth suddenly and is executed with great vigor in such a way as to produce at the same time a considerable moral effect.

If the adjustment and control of the fire of each battery on the zone which it is to attack is easy; which implies the fixing of the limits of the zones so that the lines therein (roads, railroads, paths and trails, etc.) are very visible to aerial observation.

If the expenditure of ammunition is considerable.

258. Note : When batteries are concentrated there is no less of a necessity for each battery to fire on a well defined target.

II. — NEUTRALIZING FIRE.

259. Neutralization may be obtained :

By the use of gas shells.

By the use of high explosive shells.

The use of gas shells is the most powerful means for the neutralization of the enemy and if their use is sufficiently prolonged they may accomplish the destruction of his personnel. Gas shells should be employed in preference to high explosive shells whenever atmospheric conditions are favorable (the subject of the rules for the employment of gas shells is taken up in paragraph 286).

In neutralization with high explosive shells the firing should commence with a violent burst of fire, which is followed by slow fire in order to keep the personnel under shelter. Rapid fire can be taken up again if the hostile battery tries to reopen its fire.

In order that rapid fire may be executed from the very start, the elements of the firing data must be determined in advance with all the accuracy possible and the fire registered beforehand on a neighboring target, in order to avoid having any adjustment of fire to make after having once opened fire.

The density of the fire is of the utmost importance, it is therefore of advantage to use rapid fire material as much as possible : 7 mm. guns whenever the range will permit, 105's for the longer ranges; 95's, 120's and 155's are used as well, in the order named.

III. — DESTRUCTION OF WIRE ENTANGLEMENTS.

260. The barbed wire entanglement of the necessary defenses should be opened in large breaches and not by small openings.

261. *a)* **Field Artillery.**

Fire for the destruction of wire entanglements is precise

fire. The four pieces of the battery are employed on the same breach : they are laid in direction in such a way that the same planes of fire of the separate pieces are separated by about 5 or 6 meters along the line of the wire. In this way the battery should open a breach of about 25 meters.

To make a battery breach in an entanglement about 15 to 20 meters deep and on level ground, the mean expenditure of ammunition will be as follows :

    at 2500 meters . . . .   600 shells.
    at 3000 meters   700   „
    at 4000 meters   600   „
    at 5000 meters   1000   „
    at 7000 meters   1200   „

If the entanglement is more than 30 meters deep it will be necessary to increase the above allowances by 400 shells for each 30 meters of increase in depth of the entanglement.

If the ground slopes upward toward the enemy's position the figures can be reduced.

If the ground slopes down toward the enemy (counter slope) they should be multiplied by ratio of the angle of fall to the difference between that angle and the angle of the slope of the ground. This being the case the employment of reduced charges will permit an increase in the angle of fall and a consequent reduction in the necessary increase in ammunition allowance (*).

The high explosive shell is the one to employ.

The choice of fuse depends on the character of the ground and the range. On normal ground and at ranges less than 4000 meters the best results will be obtained with I (instantaneous) or S. R. (non-delayed action) fuses; beyond 4000 meters fuses I. A. (long instantaneous) and R. Y. should be employed. In clayey soil or ground wet or softened by rain the A. R. fuse should be used as it gives low bursts on ricochet which are in general superior to the others.

(*) Reduced charges have the added advantage of lessening the wear on the guns and accordingly allowing a greater rapidity of fire; they should be employed whenever possible.

262. *b*) Trench Artillery.

The projectiles fired from trench artillery are very effective against wire entanglements when they are equipped with non-delay action or instantaneous fuses. The 58 mm. No. 2 mortar is the one chiefly employed with L. S. or D. L. S. bombs; also the 58 mm. Van Deuren mortar and the 150 mm. mortar.

In order to get the surest results in making breaches it is better to fire from directly in front of the wire.

In order to open a breach 40 meters long in an entanglement about 30 meters deep it is necessary to allow for an expenditure of :

120 large bombs
or 200 to 250 small bombs.

The matter of range and slope of ground have little influence. The 58 mm., No. 2 mortar or the Van Deuren should be employed against enemy entanglements on the counter slope of the first line which the 75 mm. guns cannot reach. If observation of fire is impossible, zone fire may be employed, of course providing for a very large consumption of ammunition.

263. *c*) Heavy Artillery.

Heavy artillery should be used only for attacking entanglements which are so well defiladed or which are at such a great range that the Field Artillery and the trench artillery cannot reach them.

Defiladed entanglements at too great a range to be attacked by the trench artillery are attacked with the 155 mm. howitzer.

In this case the D or long shell should be used with the I. A. (long instantaneous) fuses, at a range of 3000 meters. Breaches 4 or 5 meters long have been obtained in entanglements having a depth of 20 meters, whether reinforced or not with "abatis" or "trou de loups", by the use of 50 long shells or 60 D shells, under favorable conditions of fire and observation.

As with the light artillery and the trench artillery, it is

better to concentrate the means at hand, firing by battery in order to make a large breach, and not using isolated pieces. From this it will be seen that an expenditure of 200 long shells or of 300 D shells should give a breach of 20 to 25 meters long and should aid also in the disorganization of the trenches immediately in rear of the entanglement.

The entanglements at too great a range to be attacked by the howitzers will be attacked by the 155 mm. gun (the rules should be followed as for the 155 mm. howitzer, except that a greater expenditure of ammunition should be counted on).

At a range of 6000 meters 80 long shells or 100 D shells should be provided in order to obtain the same results as those given above for the 155 mm. howitzer at a range of 3000 meters; which gives the total amount of 300 long shells or 400 D shells for a battery breach, provided that observation of fire is possible.

The 105 mm. gun and the guns of a calibre larger than the 155 mm. are not to be employed against wire entanglements.

IV. — DESTRUCTION OF " CHEVAUX DE FRISE ".

264. Chevaux de frise are particularly difficult to destroy when they are well made; it being necessary to get direct hits on the target in order to destroy them.

The methods of attacking them will vary with the range and the thoroughness of the defilading :

With the 75 mm. high explosive shell, without delayed action (non-delay action or instantaneous fuse), if the chevaux de frise are not very solidly constructed.

With 58 mm. bombs, fired with P. R. fuses, with or without delayed action.

With the 155 mm. gun or howitzer shells, fired with and without delayed action.

It will be necessary to provide for an expenditure of ammunition the same as for an ordinary wire entanglement of double the depth.

V. — DESTRUCTION OF MACHINE GUN SHELTERS.

265. Machine gun shelters may be attacked either by light artillery, trench artillery or heavy artillery.

266. *a)* **Light Artillery.**

Generally speaking the light artillery cannot totally destroy these shelters. It can often knock to pieces the shelters which are made of logs but it should above all try to make direct hits on the machine gun embrasures.

To obtain the above result it will be necessary to fire with precision about a hundred high explosive shells with non-delayed action fuses.

267. *b)* **Heavy Artillery.**

The 155 mm. howitzer, the 220 mm. mortar, and the 270 mm. and 280 mm. mortars are particularly adapted to the destruction of shelters.

Generally speaking, to disorganize :

A shelter made with three layers of logs, 2 direct hits with the 155 mm. shell (long shell or D shell) are necessary.

A more solidly constructed shelter, 2 direct hits from a 220 mm., 270 mm. or 280 mm. mortar are necessary.

To obtain the above result it is necessary to fire :

70 to 80 shots from the 155 mm. howitzer, the 220, 270, or 280;

80 to 100 shots from the 155 mm. gun.

This last piece is only employed in exceptional cases, and then with a slight charge, in order to obtain a proper angle of fall.

268. *c)* **Trench Artillery.**

Trench artillery can destroy shelters by employing delayed action fuses. The number of rounds necessary in order to get two direct hits on the target is :

100 small bombs,

70 to 80 large bombs.

The best results are obtained with the D. L. S. bomb which gives an effect similar to the 220 mm. F.A. shell. This bomb is not large enough if the shelter is protected by more than 3 meters of earth. In this case it will be necessary to employ 240 mm. bombs (70 to 80 rounds).

VI. — DESTRUCTION OF TRENCHES.

269. *a*) **Light Artillery.**

The 75 mm. gun has small effect on trenches attacked from the front.

On the other hand, in the case of communication trenches taken in enfilade or under oblique fire an expenditure of 10 high explosive shells per linear meter of trench will give important results.

An effort will be made to get steep angles of fall by the employment of reduced propelling charges or by firing at longer ranges.

270. *b*) **Heavy Artillery.**

The most appropriate calibre for the destruction of trenches is the 155 mm. howitzer.

Do not try for a uniform destruction along the whole length of the trench, but concentrate on the most important points : such as places where communications come together, shelters, command posts, machine gun emplacements, places for flanking fire, etc...

To arrive at the above result, fire 80 to 100 long shells from the 155 mm. howitzer, with well observed fire, on each one of the above mentioned points.

If these points are chosen about 30 meters apart in a trench fired on from the front, and about 50 to 60 meters apart in a trench fired in enfilade, the trench should be destroyed under good conditions. This will lead to an expenditure of about :

3 rounds of 155 mm. long shells with delayed action fuse, for each linear meter of trench fired on from the front;

and 1.5 rounds per meter for trenches taken in enfilade.

With the F. A. shell the allowance should be increased by one fourth.

Enfilade fire is, then, much more economical than frontal fire. However if oblique fire is easier to get it is to be preferred to enfilade fire.

It is possible that the allowances given above may be insufficient, if it is a question of destroying large trenches. In that case the allowance will have to be increased. It is useful to know however, that timed fire with shrapnel will produce important effects on the personnel occupying parallel trenches, even if the line of fire is normal to the general trace of the trenches.

Particularly solid works, with deep dugouts or concrete protected shelters are fired with heavy calibre shells with greatly delayed action fuses (220, 270, 280, 370, 400).

271. c) Trench Artillery.

The above rules are applicable; 80 to 100 bombs being fired, small or large according to the strength of the object to be demolished. P.R. delayed action fuses should be employed by preference.

The most powerful effect is obtained with winged bombs and with 240 mm. bombs.

Trenches or communicating trenches, taken in enfilade, are torn up for a length of 100 meters by :

300 small bombs (58 mm. or Van Deuren).

This allowance will have to be increased for large trenches.

272. d) Safety zone.

The safety zone within which infantry must be forbidden to enter during the fire of the 155 mm. howitzers is at least 200 meters long, moreover it will be necessary to shelter the troops farther back from shell bursts which may fall there.

VII. — DESTRUCTION OF PERMANENT FORTIFICATION WORKS.

273. The various heavily concreted portions of the works (concrete block turrets, observation stations and watch towers, concreted shelters in the ramparts and subterranean barracks, casemates for canon and sponsons flanking the trenches, concreted communication galleries) are taken separately under fire by 293 mm., 370 mm., and 400 mm. mortars firing demolition shells with a base delayed action fuse. The ranges at which this is undertaken should be not more than three fourths of the maximum range of the piece.

The moats are filled in by the enfilade fire of the medium and heavy calibers (155 mm. gun, 240 mm., 32 cm.) directed slightly in front or in the rear of the trench in order to throw the dirt into it. This fire is done with heavily charged shells with delayed action fuses.

The destruction of the upper works is accomplished as is laid down for the destruction of trenches (155 mm. gun or 155 mm. howitzer according to the range, firing with delayed action fuses).

The entrances and routes of communication are attacked by the small and medium calibres, either with time fire or with the instantaneous fuse.

274. AMMUNITION ALLOWANCES TO BE PROVIDED.

TARGETS	CALIBERS	ALLOWANCE
Shelter in the ramparts, observation posts, emplacements for canon.	280 to 400	100 rounds for each target at ranges less than 9 kilometers and 150 rounds at greater ranges.
Casemates, and large underground storerooms	280 to 400	150 to 200 rounds per target according as the range is less or greater than 9 kilometers.
Armoured turrets.	32, 370, 400	150 rounds per target.
Armoured batteries	32, 370, 400	400 to 500 rounds.
Concreted passage ways . . .	280 to 400	100 to 150 rounds per passage with enfilade fire.
Ditches	155 gun, 240, 32	150 rounds of enfilade fire for each ditch.

VIII. — DESTRUCTION OF CERTAIN LOCALITIES.

275. The destruction of localities includes :

The breaking in of vaults of cellars;

The demolition and firing of houses;

The destruction of special work done by the enemy.

The vaults of cellars are broken in by the fire of howitzers or mortars (270, 280, 293, 370, 400) firing heavily charged shells with delayed action fuses.

If the roofs of the cellars are very strong one should use armor piercing shells with a base delayed action fuse.

The destruction of the cellars should be taken up before that of the houses in order that the debris from the latter may not form a protective layer over the former.

The destruction of houses is accomplished by an alternate fire of high explosive shells with delayed action fuse (155 mm. howitzers or 155 mm. guns, 220 or 270 mm. mortars or trench guns) and incendiary shells (155) with low time bursts.

Commence with fire with high explosive shells, continue with incendiary shells and finish with high explosive shells.

Special works of the enemy are destroyed as has been laid down for trenches and shelters.

276. AMMUNITION ALLOWANCE TO BE PROVIDED.

NATURE OF THE TARGET.	CALIBERS.	ALLOWANCES to be provided for each 100 square meters of massed houses (*).
Demolition of cellars . . .	270 to 400	4 rounds.
Destruction of houses	H. A. 155 to 270 T. M. 58 to 240	4 rounds, 1/4 incendiary.
(*) And not for the total area of the village.		

IX. — CONDUCT OF DESTRUCTION WORK.

277. Almost all the methodical destructive work preceding an attack will have to be interrupted at night (or in case of fog) on account of the impossibility of observation.

It is indispensable that the enemy should not make any repairs during the night.

In order to assure this, the whole front of the area to be destroyed should be systematically kept under fire by irregular salvoes, utilizing for this work the small and medium calibres (75, 95, 105, 120 gun) either with percussion fire, with instantaneous fuses or with time fire (shrapnel or high explosive shell).

Proceed in the same manner, night and day, for the destructive work terminated before the attack.

Provide for this work an allowance of about 300 rounds for each 200 meters of front to be attacked for a period of twelve hours.

X. — DESTRUCTION OF RAILWAYS.

278. The most important points to destroy are :

Engineering works (bridges and culverts).

The parts of the track on embankments.

Railway yards (water tanks, switch, towers, etc.).

Enfilade fire is executed whenever possible with guns of medium or heavy caliber or with howitzers throwing heavy bursting charges.

Use a shell with a big bursting charge and a delayed action fuse.

ALLOWANCE OF AMMUNITION TO BE PROVIDED.		
Targets.	Calibres.	Allowance.
Bridge or viaduct	270 to 400	200 to 100 rounds according to calibre.
Embankment.	145, 155 gun, 240	600 rounds. 400 —
Switches.	145, 155 gun, 240	400 rounds 200 —
Yards	14	200 rounds.

The above allowances apply only to enfilade fire.

If frontal fire is necessary quadruple the allowance.

XI. — FIRE ON COMMUNICATIONS.

279. The material to employ is the 75, 105, 14, 145, 155, G. P. F., 16.

This fire does not give truly good results unless it is kept up.

Effort should be made to get enfilade fire or fire at a sharply oblique angle.

Day. Continuity of the barrage is only assured by the permanence of aerial observation and by having designated beforehand batteries which should open fire upon notification from the observer.

Night. It is necessary to fire on roads and cross roads with irregular salvoes at the rate of :

About 80 rounds per hour for the 75 mm. guns.

About 40 rounds per hour for the heavy artillery.

If the target is taken in enfilade, a certain length or section of the road to be interfered with should be attacked each time.

Certain kinds of gas shells will give important results in close country (*), such as ravines and woods; on account

---

(*) Especially to be noted is the efficiency of fire on perishable supplies such as rations whenever they may be found in course of transportation. This fire to be with gas shells.

of their persistent action, lachrymatory shells may render useless certain very necessary roads.

XII. — BARRAGES.

280. The following information may be made to serve as a base for the establishment of the barrages :

281. Width of the cone of dispersion effective against personnel :

High explosive percussion shell (ricochet fire) about 15 meters.
High explosive time shell   "   20   "
Time shrapnel   "   20   "

282. Rate of fire of the 75 mm. gun.

The maximum rate of fire of the 75 is six shots per piece per minute. It is only in exceptional cases that this rate can be exceeded.

Where the duration of the fire is to be for more than 5 minutes, the rate of fire will have to be reduced in order to be able to give to the piece the care necessary for its proper conservation.

The rapidy of fire may be doubled with reduced charges.

283. *The putting down of barrages.*

The depth of the danger zone, in rear of the mean point of fall of the 75 mm. projectiles, for certain ranges, is as follows (*) :

Moving Barrage :

High explosive percussion shell. . { from 150 at 2000 m. to 200 at 5000 m.

High explosive time shell (**) . . { from 200 at 2000 m. to 250 at 5000 m.

Time shrapnel (**) . . . . { from 150 at 2000 m. to 200 at 5000 m.

(*) The danger zone is calculated in such a manner that no shell fragments shall be thrown to the rear of a vertical plane passing through the friendly first line and that none of the trajectories shall pass lower than 4 meters vertically above this line.

(**) The danger zone is figured with reference to the mean point of burst.

Fixed barrage. (The infantry being sheltered in a trench.)

Follow the above figures except for the ones for the high explosive percussion shell, the danger zone for which may be reduced 50 meters.

Remarks.

If the ground slopes up toward the enemy's position, the figures may be reduced in the case of percussion fire.

If the ground slopes down toward the enemy's position the figures will have to be raised, above all if it is a question of shrapnel fire at short ranges.

In case of falling ground, it will be advantageous :

To employ reduced charges, or (in order to increase the angle of fall) to increase the range.

To have recourse to enfilade fire.

These latter methods of fire are equally to be sought if the distance separating the friendly and enemy trenches is less than the depth of the danger zone for barrage fire normal to the front.

284. *The particular case of enfilading barrages.*

The safety zone to arrange for between our infantry and the center of impact of time or percussion fire is as follows for all ranges.

High explosive shell. . . . . 80 meters.
Time shrapnel . . . . 60 meters.

285. *Density of barrages.*

The moving barrage should have the maximum density compatible with the material at one's disposal and the duration of the attack. In order to be effective, it should not be less than two rounds per minute for each 15 meters.

The fixed barrage may have a rapid and a slow rate of fire :

In the first case its density should be two rounds per minute for each 15 meters; and in the second case the density varies with circumstances.

XIII. — GAS SHELLS.

286. Gas shells contain poisonous liquids, tear-producing liquids or a, combination of poisonous and tear-producing liquids. The efficiency of the poisonous liquids disappears very shortly after the explosion. The action of the tear producing poisonous liquids and that of the tear producing liquids may, on the contrary, persist for several days in the neighborhood of the point of burst.

287. A) RADIUS OF ACTION.

Poison gas shells. — The dimensions of the cloud burst which is instantaneously produced by the explosion are :

For the 75 . . . .   16 cubic meters.
For the 155 F.A.. . . . . . . 1000 cubic meters.
For the 58. . . . . 1300 cubic meters.

On level ground and if the atmospheric conditions are favorable, the cloud is effective for a diameter of 50 meters for the 75 and 100 meters for the other calibres.

Tear-producing poison shells. — The area covered by the vapor resulting from the explosion of the projectile is :

For the 75 . . . .   5 square meters.
For the 155F.A.. . . . .   50 square meters.

The efficiency of gas shells depends in a large measure on the atmospheric conditions. No results will be obtained with gas shells in a heavy rain.

The wind rapidly dissipates the gas clouds and accelerates the evaporation of the vapor resting on the ground. If the velocity of the wind, at the target, is more than 3 meters per second, shells can produce only a neutralizing effect.

From the point of view of efficiency the best conditions are found if the target is located in close country or in a wooded hollow and consequently sheltered from the wind. Gas shells produce neutralizing or destructive effect.

Destruction is arrived at by a rapid fire of short duration, executed for surprise effect and having for its object the surrounding of the adversary with a cloud of sufficient density before he has time to protect himself with his mask. Destruction can be obtained also by the use of the above method after a slow and prolonged fire which will have used up the protective materials in the masks.

Neutralization results from the unavoidable fatigue which is caused by the wearing of masks by the personnel which is carrying on, in the given locality, severe labor (particularly the cannoneers of the heavy batteries). This result may be obtained with an irregular fire, relatively slow, but drawn out through several hours.

By reason of the persistency of their action, tear-producing-poison shells and tear-producing shells are particularly efficient for the purposes of neutralization; but employed alone, tear-producing shells have little effect on the morale of the enemy.

During neutralization fire it is of advantage to mix in some salvoes of shrapnel or of high explosive time or percussion shell. These salvoes have a chance of reaching an enemy insufficiently sheltered or of making him take off his mask.

The mixing (*) up of fire with poison shells, poison-tear-producing shells and tear-producing shells is equally likely to surprise an enemy and to cause him losses.

Gas shells are most often used for the neutralization of batteries, giving the best results for this purpose. They may also assist in the interruption of communications in a locality favorable to their action.

But the use of such fire against indefinite or too extended targets must be avoided, especially targets which cannot be attacked with a sufficient density. *One cannot hope to get results from fire conducted in such a manner.*

(*) This mixing may be obtained, for example, by interspersing salvoes or volleys of tear-producing shells in the fire of poison shells, or the inverse; there is nothing to be gained by employing at the same time different kinds of projectiles in the same salvo or volley.

288. CONDITIONS OF SAFETY.

1st. *Poison gas.* — When the target of the battery firing poison gas shells is more than 500 meters from our lines, there is no deadly effect to be feared by our troops, whatever be the direction of the wind or the form of the ground.

When the target of the battery firing poison gas shells is less than 500 meters from our lines and when the form of the ground and the wind may cause the clouds of gas to come back on our troops, the personnel endangered by the fire should make use of their protective apparatus.

2nd. *Poison-tear-producing and tear-producing gas.* — When the target to be attacked is at a distance of more than 500 meters from our lines, no troublesome effect on our troops need be expected, whatever the direction of the wind or form of the ground, from the tear-producing shells.

The poison-tear-producing shells and the tear-producing shells should not be fired at targets situated at less than 500 meters from our lines on account of the persistency of the liquids which they contain and the possible variation in the direction of the wind.

PRINTED BY BERGER-LEVRAULT, NANCY (M.-ET-M.)

The present Instruction annuls :

1. — The Instruction of January 26, 1916, on the offensive combat of large units.

2. — The Instruction of December 16, 1916, on the object and conditions of a general offensive action.

It must be :

Neither developed,

Nor cut,

Nor paraphrased (*).

Its terminology must be strictly and exclusively employed.

(*) Any request for modification to the present Instruction must be addressed through the proper military channels to the Commander-in-Chief, who will pass on it.